# Does the European Social Model Have a Future?

## Challenges and Responses 70 years after the Beveridge Report

Edited by
Brigid Reynolds, s.m.
Seán Healy, s.m.a.

**Social Justice Ireland**

I.S.B.N. No: 978-1-907501-07-4
First Published: July 2012

Published by:
Social Justice Ireland
Working to build a just society

Social Justice Ireland
Arena House
Arena Road
Sandyford
Dublin 18
Ireland

Tel: 01-213 0724

e-mail: **secretary@socialjustice.ie**
website: **www.socialjustice.ie**

# TABLE OF CONTENTS

# CONTRIBUTORS

**Anna Coote** is Head of Social Policy at the New Economics Foundation (London)

**Tony Fahey** is Head of Social Policy at the School of Applied Social Science, University College Dublin

**Seán Healy** is Director, *Social Justice Ireland*

**Ide Kearney** is Associate Research Professor at the Economic and Social Research Institute (Dublin)

**Michelle Murphy** is Research and Policy Analyst with *Social Justice Ireland*

**Brigid Reynolds** is Director, *Social Justice Ireland*

**Yannick Vanderborght** is Professor of Political Science at the University of Saint Louis in Brussels and Visiting Professor at the Catholic University of Louvain, Belgium

**Philippe Van Parijs** is Professor at the Faculty of economic, social and political sciences of the University of Louvain (UCL) and Director of the Hoover Chair of Economic and Social Ethics.

# INTRODUCTION

This publication coincides with the 70th anniversary of the launch of the Beveridge Report which played a key role in the development of the European Social model following World War II. This model transformed Western Europe following a half century that had seen some of the worst violence in human history.

The value and sustainability of the European Social Model has been questioned in recent years. Its viability has been under much scrutiny in the context of the current economic and social crisis. Many questions have been raised concerning how it can be financed with the current focus on fiscal tightening.

A Social Model, European or otherwise, is not an end in itself. It is a means to an end. In reflecting on the European Social Model, therefore, it is important to address the issue of purpose: if there is to be a Social Model what should its purpose be? To serve that purpose what should be its shape in the future? What are the challenges faced by the European Social Model in seeking to achieve that purpose? What should be the key components of the European Social Model in the twenty first century if it's to achieve its purpose? These are key questions that must be considered.

At the European level there has been a steady process of economic integration over recent decades. While there has been a rhetorical commitment to ensuring a 'Social Europe', in reality there has been a down-grading of the place of the European Social Model over the past two decades and more. The difference between the legally binding regulatory systems and institutions underpinning economic development on the one hand, and the lack of any similar structure for social development on the other hand, illustrates this difference very clearly and highlights the relative priority of economic and social policy within an EU context.

Since 2008 the world's economy has been in turmoil. The world's political structures have failed to deal with this turmoil in a fair and just manner. This has been especially obvious within the EU. Yet the failure for the most part to address the future in anything more than economic and fiscal terms displays a profound lack of awareness of the issues at stake. Of course the economic issues are very important but so are the political, the cultural, the social and the environmental.

There is an urgent need for discussion of the vision of the future that is guiding decision-making across the board. Central to that vision at an EU level is the European Social Model. It needs to be re-imagined and re-invigorated in a manner appropriate to the twenty first century.

The chapters in this book, which were first presented at a policy conference on the topic of *Does the European Social Model have a future? – Challenges and Responses 70 years after the Beveridge Report*, seek to address some of the key questions and issues that emerge in this context. We trust readers will find them of some benefit particularly at a time of growing discussion concerning the shape of the future.

This publication is the 24th volume in this series organised and published by *Social Justice Ireland* (previously published by *CORI Justice*) which has sought to address these questions and issues on a day to day basis.

*Social Justice Ireland* expresses its deep gratitude to the authors of the various chapters that follow. They contributed long hours and their obvious talent to preparing these chapters.

*Social Justice Ireland* is concerned with issues of principles, paradigms and guiding values as well as with the specifics of problems and policies. It approaches all of these from a social justice perspective seeking at all times to tackle the causes of problems. In presenting this volume we do not attempt to cover all the questions that arise around this topic. This volume is offered as a contribution to the ongoing public debate around these and related issues.

Brigid Reynolds
Seán Healy
July 3rd, 2012

# Part One

## Challenges to the European Social Model

# 1
## Economic Challenges

## Ide Kearney[1]

## 1. Introduction

The Irish economy is facing extremely challenging times as a result of the global economic recession which began in 2008. The effects of this recession in Ireland have been greatly exacerbated because of past policy mistakes that allowed a major property market bubble to develop and also permitted the banking system to become overexposed to the property sector. The consequences have been a severe contraction in output, a major financial crisis and the rapid emergence of high rates of unemployment. Due to the collapse in economic activity in Ireland over the period 2008 to 2010 and the associated rise in unemployment, economic output per head had fallen back to its 2000 level by the end of 2011[2].

In this talk I want to concentrate on the twin challenges of very high debt levels and a very high unemployment rate that form the core of the lasting legacy of the economic crisis. Because of a growing dependence of the public finances on transaction taxes in the property sector in recent years, the severe economic shock had a catastrophic impact on the

---

[1] Economic and Social Research Institute, Dublin, Ireland. This *paper was prepared for the Social Justice Ireland Conference* 2012, **July 3rd, 2012. The material included in this paper draws on work contained in Fitz Gerald and Kearney (2011)** *Irish Government Debt and Implied Debt Dynamics: 2011-2015*, ESRI,, Bergin, A., FitzGerald, J., Kearney, I. and C. O'Sullivan, 2011, "The Irish Fiscal Crisis", *National Institute Economic Review*, No. 217, July 2011, p. R47-R59, **and a presentation I made on October 13th 2011 to an OECD LEED conference.**

[2] Using real GNP per head as a measure.

---

public finances. Government borrowing shot up to 14 per cent of GDP in 2009, having averaged a small surplus on the public finances over most of the period 2000-7, and was 13 per cent of GDP in 2011[3]. Cumulative government direct intervention in the banking system was equivalent to 37 per cent of GDP in 2011, while contingent liabilities related to the banking system are currently estimated at over 110 per cent of GDP. The explosion in government debt has led to domestic and international concerns as to the sustainability of Irish government debt over the medium-term.

Along with this debt crisis, the Irish labour market has deteriorated rapidly during the recession. The unemployment rate has increased from below 5 per cent to almost 15 per cent, with a strong growth in long-term unemployment and a steady fall in active participation in the labour market.

The policy challenges facing the authorities in tackling the debt and unemployment crises are considerable. During the previous unemployment of the 1980s, the authorities were forced to implement a severe programme of fiscal consolidation despite a mounting unemployment problem. Unfortunately we find ourselves facing the same policy dilemma today, despite high unemployment the authorities are forced to implement pro-cyclical policies which serve to deepen the recession.

## 2. Double Trouble: Twin Housing and Credit Bubbles

The Irish economy enjoyed an exceptional period of sustained growth from 1994 through to the early years of the last decade. This was largely driven by the expansion in world trade and a rapid increase in world market share for Irish exports. The rapid rise in employment and incomes together with the increased availability of low cost finance as a

---

[3]    Excluding the once-off costs of the banking crisis, the respective deficits are 11½ per cent in 2009 and 9½ per cent in 2011.

consequence of EMU membership and the globalisation of the financial sector resulted in a boom in the building and construction sector in the last decade, in particular a rapid expansion in house building. As shown in Figure 1, housing investment peaked at 13 per cent of GNP in 2006, more than double the EU-15 average. This housing boom drove economic growth over the "bubble" years from 2003 onwards so that the level of actual output rose well above the potential of the economy to deliver.

**Figure 1: The housing bubble and credit bubble.**

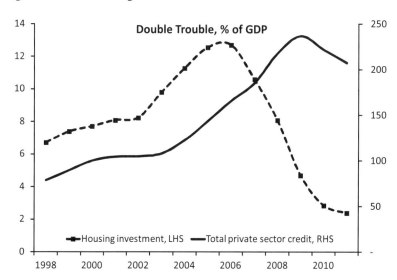

Source: CSO National Accounts and Central Bank Quarterly Bulletins, own calculations.

The second strand of the emerging bubble can be seen in the explosion in private sector credit which increased from 100 per cent of GDP in 2002-2003 to well over 230 per cent of GDP by 2009 (Figure 1). This dramatic increase in bank lending was financed abroad. While domestic savings were sufficient to fund the housing boom up to around 2003, thereafter they proved increasingly inadequate. Instead, the banking sector financed the boom by borrowing increasing sums abroad and relending these funds domestically to the property sector.

The first "conventional" early warning indicator of this growing domestic imbalance was the balance of payments, where the big increase in investment in housing was reflected in a growing deficit on the current account of the balance of payments, matched by a growing surplus on the financial account which reflected the foreign borrowing by the banking sector (Figure 2). The deficit on the current account began to deteriorate from 2003 onwards, a much earlier indicator of looming danger than output, employment or public finance indicators.

**Figure 2: Early warning indicator**

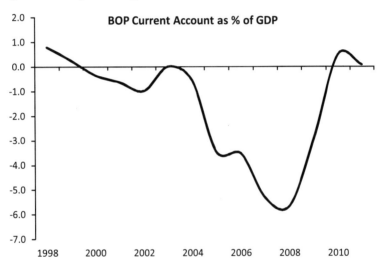

Source: CSO Balance on International Payments, own calculations.

The bursting of these bubbles has caused significant damage to the economy both in terms of measured economic activity and in employment. Whether measured by GDP or GNP, the latest quarterly data suggest that measured output in 2011 is at levels last seen in 2003 or 2004[4] (Figure 3) while the unemployment rate has soared from below 5 per cent of the active labour force in 2007 to almost 15 per cent by early 2012 (Figure 4).

---

[4]  As mentioned earlier, real GNP per capita is currently at 2000 levels, the fall is even larger since the population has increased over the period.

## Figure 3: Collapse in output and incomes and labour market

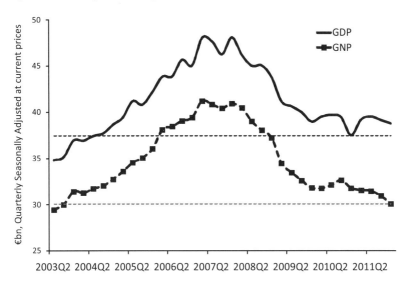

## Figure 4: Collapse in labour market

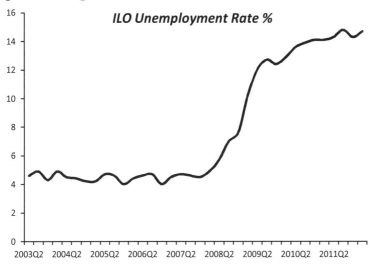

Source: CSO Quarterly National Account and CSO Quarterly National Household Survey.

# 3. An Explosive Debt Crisis

The collapse in the property market bubble, the resulting implosion of the domestic banking system and the associated huge fall in domestic output led to a dramatic growth in government indebtedness over the last four years. Having been one of the EU economies with the lowest government debt burden in 2007, Ireland has moved to being one of the more heavily indebted economies with gross government debt estimated at 108 per cent of GDP in 2011.

**Figure 5: Deficit**

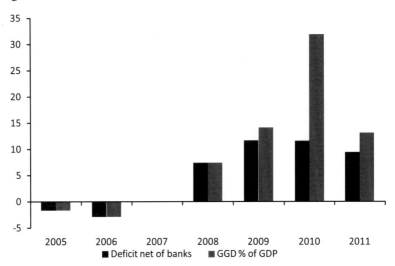

The very rapid deterioration in the fiscal position from 2007 onwards (Figure 5), together with significant transfers of funds to the banking system and injections of capital into the banks meant that by the end of 2011 gross and net government debt amounted to 108 per cent of GDP and 96 per cent respectively. Figure 5 shows the General Government Deficit (GGDP) as a % of GDP. These deficit figures in 2009-2011 include funding of the banking system. While it is necessary to exclude "once-off"

effects of banking internventions to arrive at the "underlying" deficit, these banking interventions have had a significant effect on the measured deficit in every year since 2009, this annual recurrences raises issues about them being treated as once-off.

**Figure 6: Gross and Net Debt**

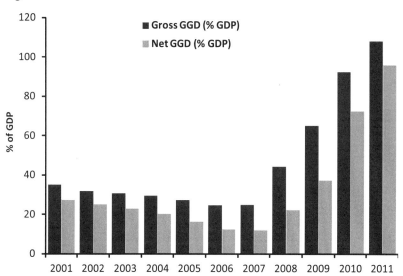

Over the period 2000 to 2007 Irish government debt was low and falling (see Figure 6). In 2001 the government set up the National Pension Reserve Fund (NPRF) and 1 per cent of GNP was invested each year in that fund to provide for future pension requirements. The value of the fund grew rapidly to €21 billion in 2007. Along with cash balances and surpluses on a number of other managed funds, these investments meant that the gap between gross and net government debt grew steadily between 2001 and 2007, from 8 percentage points of GDP in 2001 to 13 percentage points of GDP in 2007. In 2008 the Irish authorities pre-funded future deficits by borrowing significant additional sums so that liquid assets – in the form of both cash holdings and the NPRF – amounted to almost half of total gross government debt (Figure 5).

In 2009 the government decided that some of the assets of the National Pension Reserve Fund (NPRF) could be used to recapitalise troubled banks. These are referred to as "directed investments". Effectively these NPRF assets were made available to the exchequer to help fund the government deficit and bank recapitalisations. The total value of the NPRF at the end of 2011 was €14.5 billion, of which €5.4 billion was available as liquid financial assets[5].

Figure 7 shows the dramatic impact that direct government intervention in the banking system since the beginning of 2009 has had on the government debt figures. By the end of 2011 total gross government debt stood at €169 billion. Just over half of that, €87 billion, is due to the "fiscal debt", that is the effect of the cumulation of fiscal deficits on the original total stock of debt. A further €19 billion of it is due to the strategy of holding significant liquid financial assets, in the form of cash and discretionary funds held at the NPRF. A staggering 37 per cent of total government debt relates to the government's direct intervention in the banking system. This is equivalent to €63 billion, of which €35.6 billion was a direct transfer or in other words a direct loss to the exchequer.

In late summer 2010 the government still expected to be able to fund itself on financial markets. However as the full magnitude of the potential losses in in the banking system began to be apparent in the autumn of 2010, the government had to seek aid from the IMF/EU towards the end of 2010. One of the key factors driving nervousness in the markets at that time was the scale of contingent liabilities related to the banking system that are not included in the official debt figures.

---

[5]    At the end of 2011 €9.1 billion was in the "Directed Portfolio" of investments in Allied Irish Bank and Bank of Ireland and it is, therefore, excluded from liquid financial assets.

## Figure 7: Fiscal and Bank Debt

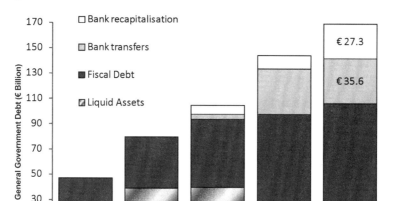

There are three main sets of government liabilities in relation to the banking system: liabilities that are included in the Government debt relating to direct intervention by the government in the banking system as shown in Figure 7; contingent liabilities arising from NAMA bonds backed by property assets; residual contingent liabilities arising from the government guarantee of the bulk of covered banks' liabilities. Table 1 shows the most recent estimate of the total value of these contingent liabilities at 112 per cent of GDP. While there is a degree of clarity about these contingent liabilities of the State there is considerable uncertainty about the future value of the offsetting financial assets held by the covered institutions. The scale of the State's contingent liabilities in the banking system relative to the actual size of the Irish economy is very large. In this sense the State is highly geared.

**Table 1: Contingent Liabilities**

|  | % of 2011 GDP |
|---|---|
| Senior NAMA bonds | 19% |
| Gurantees for Emergency Liquidity Assistance | 10% |
| Deposits covered by Deposit Protection Scheme | 52% |
| Bank Liabilities covered by ELG | 32% |
| Total Contingent Liabilites end March 2012 | 112% |

Source: IMF Country Report March 2012

# 4. Unemployment Crisis

The unemployment rate has grown with alarming speed since 2008, and most recent estimates suggest it is close to 15 per cent of the labour force. More worrying is that the persistence of unemployment, which can lead to the emergence of structural unemployment, is rising. Figure 8 shows the long-tem unemployment rate, that is those out of work for more than one year, has been rising steadily since 2009 and now accounts for roughly 60% of the total unemployed. Furthermore it is much higher among men, particularly young men. The legacy effects of this are the sector specific nature of unemployment, with very large falls in employment in the construction sector.

In addition to the fall in employment, there has also been a huge fall in participation in the labour market. Figure 9 shows what the measured unemployment rate would be using wider definitions of labour force participation, to include those who are more "marginally attached" to the labour market, underemployed part-time workers and those who are not in education who want work. Using the widest definition the measured unemployment rate in 2012 Q1 is 24 per cent. Figure 10 helps to clarify this issue. It shows total employment and the total labour force from peak to today. At its peak, in 2008 Q3 the total labour force included 2.267 million people. That had fallen by 172,000 to 2.095 million by 2012 Q1. This very sharp fall in labour force participation means that headline unemployment numbers are lower, however it is likely that this is capturing pent-up labour supply were labour market conditions to improve.

### Figure 8: Long Term UR

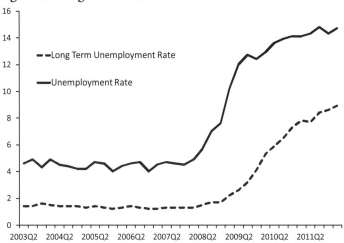

### Figure 9: The labour force

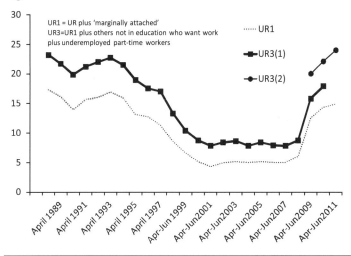

## Figure 10: Loss of Jobs during Recession

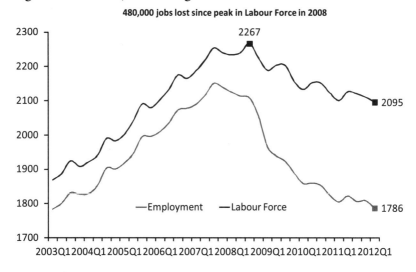

**480,000 jobs lost since peak in Labour Force in 2008**

## Figure 11: Educational profile of unemployed

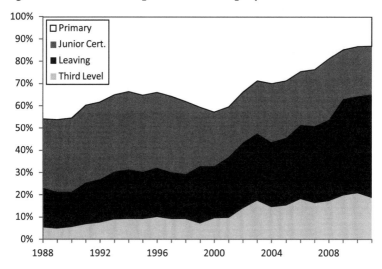

Source: QNHS PES data for Q2 in each year, own calculations.

Figure 11 shows that the educational profile of the unemployed has changed radically from the 1980s. In 1988 23% of those unemployed had the Leaving Certificate or higher, whereas now this is 65%. This changes the sort of interventions and training programmes required, and paints a slightly more optimistic picture of what the future will hold as the economy recovers as the higher the education level the better employment prospects are.

# 5. The policy challenge: high debt and high unemployment

The depth of the fiscal crisis, coupled with mounting costs for the government from the financial crisis, forced the Irish authorities to make very significant interventions to stabilise the deficit. To date, the total amount of ex ante cuts implemented is equivalent to almost €24 billion (15 per cent of GDP), with a further €8.5 billion in cuts planned for 2013-2015.

Since the summer of 2008 the Irish fiscal position deteriorated very rapidly. Beginning in autumn 2008, the authorities responded to this deterioration with a series of austerity budgets designed to stabilise the deficit. The speed of the widening of the deficit, even in the face of these measures, warranted a supplementary budget in the spring of 2009 and it was not until 2010 that the measures undertaken were sufficient to see the deficit stabilise. Table 2 summarises the *ex ante* measures undertaken and planned. By the end of 2010 the general government deficit had stabilised, however at a very high level of 11 ½ per cent of GDP. In November 2010 the Irish government agreed a package of loans from the EU/IMF designed to help fund Irish debt over the period 2011-2013. That agreement also mapped out a further package of austerity measures designed to bring the deficit below 3 per cent of GDP by the middle of the decade.

Roughly two-thirds of the actual and planned austerity package relates to cuts in expenditure, both current and capital. In 2009 and 2010 significant cuts in public sector pay levels were introduced, equivalent to up to 15 per cent of gross salary. There have also been very large cuts in expenditure on capital projects. On the revenue side, taxes on income have risen substantially in these years. Over the period 2011-2014 the consolidation measures total €15 billion, or 10 per cent of 2010 GDP. This means that cumulatively by 2015 the Irish authorities will have introduced ex ante austerity measures equivalent to over 20 per cent of GDP.

**Table 2: The Austerity Package**

|  | 2008 | 2009 | 2010 | 2011 | 2012 | 2013 | 2014 | 2015 | Total |
|---|---|---|---|---|---|---|---|---|---|
| **Revenue** | 0.0 | 5.6 | 0.0 | 1.4 | 1.6 | 1.1 | 1.1 |  | 10.8 |
| **Expenditure** | 1.0 | 3.9 | 4.3 | 3.9 | 2.2 | 2.3 | 2.0 |  | 19.6 |
| **of which capital:** | 0.0 | 0.6 | 1.0 | 1.9 | 0.8 | 0.6 | 0.1 |  | 5.0 |
| **Total** | 1.0 | 9.4 | 4.3 | 5.3 | 3.8 | 3.4 | 3.1 | 2.0 | 32.3 |

Source : Department of Finance, various. See footnote.[6]

Figure 11 shows our estimates of the fiscal stance in Ireland over recent decades. Using the ESRI HERMES model of the Irish economy, this is estimated by comparing a scenario where both government expenditure and taxes are indexed with the actual budgetary outturn for each year. The methodology is described in Kearney *et al.* (2000)[7]. A positive difference implies an expansionary budget and a negative sign indicates a contractionary budget.

---

[6] For 2008-2010 *Report of the Review Group on State Assets and Liabilities.* [Table 2.1: Budgetary Adjustments since mid-2008 – Planned Budgetary Impact.] For 2011 and 2012 *Budget 2011, Budget 2012, Medium Term Fiscal Statement,* November 2012 Table 2.1. The figures included show the full year effects, including carryover, and exclude once-off measures. For 2013-2015 figures from *Medium Term Fiscal Statement,* November 2012 Table 2.1

[7] Kearney, I., McCoy, D., Duffy, D., McMahon, M., and D Smyth, 2000. "Assessing the Stance of Irish Fiscal Policy", in A. Barrett (ed.), Budget Perspectives: Proceedings of a Conference held on 19 September 2000, ESRI.

## Figure 12: Fiscal Stance (LHS) and GDP growth rate (RHS), annual averages.

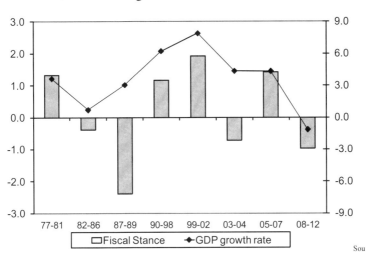

Source: own calculations.

Scanning across Figure 12 we can see that the origins of the fiscal crisis of the mid 1980s can be traced to inappropriately stimulatory fiscal policy in the late 1970s and early 1980s. While tough budgets were introduced in 1983 and 1984, the process was only completed with further very tough budgets in 1988 and 1989. A consequence of this long drawn out adjustment was a lost decade in terms of growth.

It would have been much more appropriate to have run a much tighter fiscal policy over the course of the last decade, resulting in a substantial and increasing surplus up to and including 2007. Figure 12 shows our estimate of the fiscal stance from 1977 to 2012 cumulated over successive periods of expansionary or contractionary budgetary stance. The graph also shows the average annual growth rate in those periods. At first glance it is clear that fiscal policy has been broadly pro-cyclical throughout the last three and a half decades, with the exception of the years 1987-1989 when the government introduced a successful fiscal consolidation during a period of positive growth.

What is interesting about the 2005-2007 period is the similarity in the growth rate and the magnitude of the fiscal stance to the earlier 1977-1981 period of expansion. By contrast, the subsequent fiscal consolidation of 2008-2012 has been deeper than that estimated in the period 1982-1986 when very little progress was made ex post in discretionary budgetary adjustments. In both cases, the austerity measures were introduced against a backdrop of low or negative growth and rapidly rising unemployment. The fiscal consolidation in the 1980s was only successfully completed in the latter part of the decade during a reemergence of strong growth in external demand which helped to offset the very sharp fiscal contraction of the years 1987-1989.

There are few easy options in tackling the current levels of debt facing the Irish government. The current programme of austerity, with an agreed package of cuts totalling €32 billion over the period 2008-2015, should, on official assumptions, be sufficient to all but eliminate the primary deficit by 2013. However, the very high current levels of debt mean that if growth were to prove less than assumed in the Department of Finance estimates, it would not be sufficient to stabilise the debt to GDP ratio before 2015 (see FitzGerald and Kearney (2011)).

I have earlier aluded to the dangers of a lost decade: this is especially pertinent in relation to long-term unemployment, youth unemploment and male unemployment. The crisis in the labour market means that it is not sufficient to await resolution of the debt crisis before tackling the problem of long-term unemployment, as recognised in the *Pathways to Work* initiative. My colleagues at the ESRI have done a lot of work on this: key policy initiatives to tackle long term unemployment involve the use of labour market activation measures, and education and training measures[8].

---

[8]  Submission to the *Joint Committee on Jobs, Social Protection and Education* on Unemployment and Youth Unemployment, *Elish Kelly, Seamus McGuinness and Philip O'Connell,* The Economic and Social Research Institute, April, 2012

Does the European Social Model Have a Future?

As I type these last lines I am also keeping an eye on developments in Greece, where elections are taking place today. The news stories this weekend are full of reports of further plans to accelerate fiscal integration, an emerging crisis for Italian sovereign debt and the crisis for Spanish banks. Against this backdrop of a political, economic and financial crisis in Europe, and more particularly in the Eurozone, the twin fiscal and employment crises facing Ireland are thrown into even sharper relief. There are no easy choices ahead.

# 2

## Welfare and Debt:
## Lessons from Beveridge and his Times

### *Tony Fahey*

The title of this conference invites us to look at the current problems facing the welfare state in Europe in the light of the Beveridge report, which was published in December 1942. Part of the legend of Beveridge is the excitement it caused among the public when it appeared: hundreds of people queued outside the government publication offices in London to buy a copy on the day it was published and the first print run was sold out within 24 hours (Abel-Smith 1992, Timmins 2008). Its larger claim to fame lies in the inspiration it provided for the 'cradle to the grave' welfare state that so many countries in the western world sought to create once the war was over. Welfare provisions of a recognisably modern type had been emerging across parts of Europe and the New World since the late nineteenth century but *comprehensive* programmes which sought to provide security for citizens on all core welfare needs over their whole lifetimes were a novel aspiration of this period. This aspiration came to varying degrees of fruition in the 1940s and 1950s in the countries of post-war Western Europe. It has been part of the logic of European integration that the member states share a common commitment to the legacy of that era and recognise a need to join together to underpin the 'social model' that legacy has bestowed on us. While the term 'European social model' is misleading if it is taken to mean either that EU member states have adopted similar systems of welfare provision or that the EU itself has created substantial EU-wide welfare institutions, it does have real meaning as a label for values and aspirations that were expressed seventy years ago by Beveridge and that EU member states still espouse as part of their guiding philosophy.

Today, as economic crisis drags on, welfare spending is under pressure in much of Europe and the European project itself is in greater danger of falling apart than at any time since it started, what can we learn from looking back at Beveridge and his times? Here I will pick out two things from which lessons for today can be drawn. One is the scale of the ambition which Beveridge represented and how it sought to transcend the context in which it was framed. The second relates to challenges facing European reconstruction when welfare states along Beveridgean lines began to be created once the war ended – and here, in light of current concerns with sovereign debt as a constraint on welfare spending, the question of how huge national debts built up during the war were dealt with is of interest. Different countries in Europe in this period dealt with crushing burdens of government debt in different ways and these differences seem to have had enormous consequences, not least for the growth of welfare states. Remarkably little is known about this aspect of economic history (and indeed it is striking how little attention the discipline of economics has paid to the history of debt until recent years – see esp. the pioneering work of Reinhart and Rogoff 2010). The purpose of this paper is simply to highlight some general features of the experience of that era since we need to draw on all possible sources of insight into the relationship between welfare provision and the constraints imposed by government debt as we seek to cope with the current crisis.

# The ambition

Looking back at European social and economic history in the 20th century, it is now common to refer to the years from the late 1940s to the early 1970s as a golden age – a period of strong and stable economic growth, healthy demographics and narrowing social inequalities. We also tend to think of the welfare systems of that era as an outgrowth of those benign conditions, for example, in that strong social security provision was easier to attain in what was a long period of economic expansion and virtually full employment than it became when economies stagnated and the numbers unemployed multiplied in Europe in the post-1973 years.

However, one of the first lessons we learn from looking back at Beveridge comes from recalling its date. It was written not in the early 1950s, when the sunny uplands of prosperity and social progress were already in view, but between mid-1941 and mid-1942 (Abel-Smith 1992, Timmins 2008). These were the dark days in the depths of the war when Hitler's bombing campaign had left Britain's cities in rubble and fascism had turned out the light on liberal democracy in continental Europe. And it was not just that those days were bad in themselves, rather they were but another low in a three decades-long sequence of misery that had started with the First World War in 1914, had taken a dreadful turn with the global flu epidemic of 1918-20 (which killed over 50 million people, most of them young adults – Tauenberg and Morens 2006) and had continued with the depression of the 1930s. As the war broke out in 1939, anyone who was aged in their late 20s or older had already lived through one of the most traumatic periods in modern European history. Events to come over the course of the war would justify the labelling of the first half of the twentieth century the most violent and destructive in all of human history.

A remarkable feature of the Beveridge's report, then, is that it should have emerged when it did. Europe's long night of war and destruction was still a long way from dawn and its capacity to engineer social stability and economic progress out of peacetime conditions was still unknown. In that context, Beveridge's report did not reflect the advent of a new era but was an expression of hope that a new era would eventually come. Beveridge himself approached his work in these terms: he sought to provide inspiration and courage for a beleaguered British people, not just to frame a technical plan. He had been asked, when undertaking the task, merely to provide a 'tidying up' of existing social insurance arrangements but what he determined the moment needed was radical change. As he declared, 'A revolutionary moment in the world's history is a time for revolutions, not patching up' (Beveridge 1942, p. 6). While his purpose in part was to sketch out a practical scheme of income security, he also sought to project a vision of a better future and inspire faith that such a vision could be brought to pass.

Thus it was that the detailed analysis of social insurance and social assistance which forms the bulk of the report was prefaced with a brief but powerful sketch of a 'comprehensive policy of social progress', presented in exalted, even moving language. It identified the 'five Giant Evils' on the road to reconstruction – Want, Disease, Ignorance, Squalor and Idleness. The package of measures needed to conquer these evils were also sketched: social insurance and social assistance to overcome want, health services to overcome disease, education to overcome ignorance, housing to overcome squalor, and full employment to overcome idleness. Most of the report focused on the attack on want, the centre-piece of which was a flat-rate social insurance scheme. It said little of the 'allied services' in health, education and housing that would be needed to deal with the other challenges. Nevertheless, it was the comprehensive visionary aspect of the report, the outline of the overall package of services that later were to become the pillars of the welfare state, that caught people's imagination and turned his report into a bestseller.

The key to the power of the Beveridge report, then, lies in the way it transcended the context in which it was written. Its vision of a state committed to serving the welfare needs of its population was a hopeful imagining of a different future, not a technical projection of what was feasible in the circumstances of the time. An important lesson it holds for us today lies precisely in its visionary, transcendent character and its refusal to accept that difficult current conditions should trump the principles of social solidarity by which nations should govern themselves. It denied that, apart from the cessation of war, there were other more fundamental circumstances that had to come right before the state would seek to ensure that people's core welfare needs were met. It implied, rather, that securing welfare was itself the fundamental task and was at the heart of what post-war reconstruction should mean.

We often hear our present economic difficulties referred to as 'the worst since the Depression'. While this may well be true in a narrow economic sense, to bracket the broader social and political context we have today with that which formed the backdrop to the Beveridge report is to lose perspective. High unemployment, declines in living standards and the collapse of businesses since the onset of crisis four years ago cause real distress and warrant energetic action by government. But they do not rank with the destruction and chaos, the loss of life and the sheer duration of misery that preceded and accompanied the publication of Beveridge's report.

In view of this gulf in the scale of difficulty between then and now, it would be remarkable if current economic problems were to produce what Beveridge succeeded in warding off – a relegation of social solidarity to second place in plans for reconstruction that were focused primarily on other demands, in the present instance the demands of financial markets. Beveridge was no socialist radical, in that he accepted the logic of markets and the need for welfare systems to work with rather than against market forces. But he believed that markets could thrive while serving the demands of social solidarity. That belief proved to be justified as welfare-oriented market systems were created to extraordinarily positive effect in the western countries in the post-war years. It is important today, as we struggle to restore markets to normal functioning, that we hold on to Beveridge's assumption that markets should serve human welfare and be regarded as 'normal' only when they work to achieve that goal.

## Debt and welfare state development

The first elements of the welfare state envisioned by Beveridge were already being put in place before the war ended. Universal free secondary education was made available through Butler's Education Act, passed in 1944, and a bill providing for universal children's allowances became law in June 1945, within weeks of the cessation of fighting. Labour came to power a few weeks later, in July 1945, on the promise of full implementation of the Beveridge report. Yet, for the first two years after the war, in Britain as in the rest of Europe, economic recovery was slow to emerge. Much of the austerity of the war years, including food rationing and the lack of proper housing for millions of people, persisted. By 1947, Europe's growing inability to finance its continuing huge imports of basic consumer commodities (especially food) and capital goods from the United States threatened to bring a new economic crisis. Britain in particular, faced with a run on sterling in the summer of 1947, was 'heading not for New Jerusalem but for Starvation Corner' (Newton 1984, p. 398). By 1948, however, economic take-off had commenced and the following 25 years brought the fastest rate of growth ever experienced before or since in European economic history (Eichengreen 2007). As already indicated, this upsurge in growth was not a precondition for the drive to develop welfare provision in European countries in this period, since these were already gathering steam even as economic problems intensified in 1946-47. But it did enable that drive to achieve much more than it otherwise would have done.

There were many reasons why the economic aftermath of the Second World War became so positive within such a short period, but here, by way of counterpoint to difficulties faced in Europe today, I want to focus on one aspect of the picture. This is the dire financial situation, particularly high levels of debt, faced by governments in western Europe at the end of the war and how these were dealt with, in most cases quite quickly.

By 1945, government debt in Britain and France approached 250 per cent of GDP (Taylor n.d.). In Germany, Hitler had commandeered rather than borrowed what he needed to finance the war and any debts he did incur died with him. However, debts outstanding from the 1920s and 1930s devolved largely onto the new West German government, with a portion nominally attributed to East Germany (and therefore treated as uncollectable until such time as reunification might occur – Guinnane 2004, Ritschl 2012). These legacy debts in Germany were large: they have been estimated at 300 per cent of Germany's GDP in 1938, of which the equivalent of 90 per cent of GDP consisted of foreign debt (Ritschl 2012). Responsibility for this huge financial obligation thus had the potential to be a severe burden on post-war West Germany.

In these countries, therefore, as in much of western Europe, the overhang of government debt in 1945 was enormous and was well in excess of what the most indebted countries in western Europe face today. It is therefore instructive to note how this debt burden was dealt with, and here the three countries just mentioned – Britain, France and West Germany – illustrate three of the most important methods for doing so that were available then and are still available today.

*France*
The case of France is relatively straightforward since it relied largely on a common tactic for reducing national debt – a burst of inflation. It had high inflation during and immediately after the war, peaking at 74 per cent in 1946 (Reinhart and Rogoff 2009, Table 12.3). By 1950, inflation had reduced government debt to just 40 per cent of GDP, one sixth of what it had been five years earlier, and the interest bill on that debt had fallen below 2 per cent of GDP (Taylor n.d., p. 8). This rapid shrinkage of the debt burden, followed by curtailment of inflation from the early 1950s onwards, helped lay the groundwork for French participation in the golden age of growth in the 1950s and 1960s.

*Britain*
Britain, by contrast, was keen to protect the status of sterling as a reserve currency and so struggled to avoid either direct default or indirect default through high inflation. As a result, its national debt declined much more slowly than that of other European states: by 1960, despite sustained economic growth in the 1950s, government debt still exceeded 100 per cent of British GDP (Taylor n.d. p. 19). More significantly, debt service costs remained high: the interest bill on government debt exceeded 7 per cent of GDP per annum for almost ten years after the war and hovered around 6 per cent of GDP per annum until the early 1980s. It thus represented a massive cumulative drain on British resources. This drain is regarded by some economic historians as the main macro-economic factor accounting for Britain's relatively weak economic performance in the decades after the war, especially compared to West Germany (Eichengreen and Ritschl 2008, pp. 32-3). While Britain did grow steadily during the 'golden age', its growth rate was the lowest in western Europe

and gave rise to sharp relative decline in Britain's economic standing. It was also a major constraint on social spending and is one of the reasons why, despite having produced the original vision of the welfare state in the Beveridge report, Britain developed one of the least generous of the European welfare states in the 'golden age' era.

Thus we can say that the British government's efforts to protect the status of sterling by honouring its war debt in full may have had indirect economic benefits, and may have shored up London's status as an international financial centre, but it came at great cost to the British people.

*West Germany*
This brings us to the exceptional case of West Germany. Uniquely in western Europe in this period, it obtained the benefit of generous debt forgiveness, largely brought about through the intervention of the 'benevolent hegemon' of the day, the United States. The US role in European reconstruction in the post-war years is usually identified mainly with the Marshall Plan, the programme of US aid which ran from 1948 to 1951. Through this programme, the US in effect gave European countries for free the vital imports from the US (including food) which they lacked the means to purchase. The intention was to provide temporary assistance until European economies recovered their full productive capacity and created the institutional framework – including the 'social contract' embodied in emerging welfare states – they needed to gain a stable footing (for general accounts, see Crafts 2011, Judt 2010, pp 23 ff.). The direct economic impact of this programme may have been relatively modest in much of Europe though its indirect effects through institutional development may have been more significant (Crafts 2011 surveys the main debates on this question).

In regard to West Germany, however, Ritschl (2012) has highlighted a neglected feature of US intervention in this period. This was its role in shielding West Germany from demands for debt repayment by its foreign creditors and eventually, through the London Debt Agreement of 1953, securing a write-off of over half of its foreign debt and easy repayment terms for the balance (Ritschl 2012, Guinnane 2004, pp. 27-8). By Rietschl's account, the real significance of Marshall Aid was that it enabled the US to pressurise governments in Germany's creditor countries into acquiescing to this special treatment for German debt. The US approach in turn reflected the view that West Germany was of vital strategic significance in the new Cold War era and warranted special supportive treatment for that reason . As Guinnane (2004, p. 40-1) puts it, 'the German economy was so important to the world economy, and to Europe in particular, that the country was in a strong position to demand concessions that would enable her to return quickly to her traditional role as the engine of the European economy'.

In regard to government debt, the effect of the concessions it secured was to place the new West German state in a uniquely favourable financial position. Its government debt started out at less than 25 per cent of GDP and the annual interest bill on that debt was less than half of one per cent of GDP (Taylor n.d. p. 9). The broader economic significance was the contribution this favourable debt regime made to West Germany's spectacular growth rate, which was the highest in Europe and double that of Britain in the 1950s and 1960s. Furthermore, by Eichengreen and Ritschl's account (2008, pp. 32-3), the taxes that Britain was raising in the 1950s to service its heavy debt burden were paralleled in West Germany by taxes devoted to developing its social security system. Thus the boost to the West German economy occurred alongside a commitment to social solidarity which many in Britain shared in principle but were hampered from achieving because of national subservience to the demands of debt repayment.

# The lessons

The Beveridge report was inspirational in its day because it raised people's eyes beyond the horrific constraints of war and destruction and held out a noble but attainable vision of how peace-time society should be organised. Much of the report consisted of dry, technical analysis of how a national scheme of social insurance might be designed and financed but its animating force was a conviction that social solidarity was a primary value that transcended the limitations of any particular moment. As we struggle with the problems of today, that conviction is worth re-asserting.

Steps to implement Beveridge's vision had begun to take place in Britain before the end of the war and the pace of implementation intensified when Labour came to power in Britain in 1945. Similar developments took off quickly elsewhere in western Europe at the same time. However, government debt on a scale that, relatively speaking, was much larger than that of European countries today loomed as a potential major constraint both on economic recovery and welfare development. In the event, this constraint nowhere acted as a complete block to either economic growth or the expansion of welfare provision. In most cases, it melted away and was soon forgotten – and it is remarkable today to recall that such an outcome did in fact widely occur.

Only in Britain was the national debt treated as sacrosanct and financial interests regarded as paramount. That in itself did not prevent Britain from sharing in the golden age of rising prosperity and social solidarity but it did have a strong dampening effect: Britain's performance on these fronts was among the weakest in Europe and reduced its capacity to fulfil Beveridge's vision. Britain's decision to take this route in effect meant that those who contributed cash to the war effort – financial debt – were put on an equal footing with the mass of the people who had contributed through blood and suffering – human debt. Looking from the vantage point of today the wisdom of that decision seems questionable. It also reminds us that states always have obligations to their people and these always amount to a form of human debt. It may be no more valid today to rank financial debt over human debt than it was in Britain in the 1940s. The current crises of sovereign debt afflicting Europe need to be evaluated in that light.

# References

Abel-Smith, B. (1992) 'The Beveridge Report: Its origins and outcomes' *International Social Security Review* 45, 1-2:

Beveridge, W.A. (1942) *Social Insurance and Allied Services. Report by Sir William Beveridge. Cmd. 6404.* London: His Majesty's Stationery Office

Crafts, N. (2011) 'The Marshall Plan: A reality check' Department of Economics Working Paper No. 49, University of Warwick

Eichengreen, B. (2008) *The European Economy since 1945. Coordinated Capitalism and Beyond.* Princeton: Princeton University Press

Eichengreen, B. and Ritschl, A. (2008) 'Understanding West German Economic Growth in the 1950s' Working Papers 113/08, Department of Economic History, London School of Economics

Guinnane, T. (2004) 'Financial *Vergangenheitsbewaeltigung*: The 1953 London Debt Agreement' Yale University Economic Growth Center Discussion Paper No. 880

Judt, Tony (2010) *Postwar.A History of Europe since 1945.* London: Vintage

Newton, C.C.S. (1984) 'The Sterling Crisis of 1947 and Britain's Response to the Marshall Plan' *Economic History Review* 37, 3: 391-408

Reinhart, C.M. and Rogoff, K.A. (2009) *This Time Is Different. Eight Centuries of Financial Folly.* Princeton & Oxford: Princeton University Press

Ritschl, A. (2012) 'Germany, Greece and the Marshall Plan' *The Economist*, Free Exchange blog, 15 June 2012.

Taubenberger, JK and D. M. Morens (2006) '1918 Influenza: the Mother of All Pandemics' *Emerging Infectious Diseases* 12, 1 (www.cdc.gov/eid)

Taylor, B. (n.d.) 'Paying Off Government Debt: Two Centuries of Global Experience' Global Financial Data. Available at http://www.globalfinancialdata.com/news/articles/government_debt.pdf.

Timmins, N. (2008) *Five Giants: A Biography of the Welfare State.* London: Harper Collins

# Part Two

## Responding to Key Challenges to the European Social Model

# 3

## *Basic Income in a Globalized Economy*[9]

## *Philippe Van Parijs & Yannick Vanderborght*[10]

A basic income is an income unconditionally granted to all members of a society on an individual basis, without means test or work requirement.[11] It is a form of minimum income guarantee that is unconditional in three distinct senses:

(1) individual : the right to it and its level are independent of household composition;
(2) universal : it is paid irrespective of any income from other sources, which can therefore be added to the basis it provides;
(3) free of counterpart : it is paid without requiring the performance of any work or the willingness to accept a job if offered.

Its being individual matters because of the difference it makes to intra-household relationships, because it makes intrusion into living arrangements unnecessary and because it avoids any penalty for communal living. Its being universal matters, because it guarantees a high rate of take up, because it avoids stigmatization of the beneficiaries

---

[9] Earlier versions of parts of this text were presented at the founding congress of the South Korean Basic Income Network (Seoul, January 2010), at the annual meeting of the September Group (Oxford, June 2010), at the 13th Congress of the Basic Income Earth Network (Sao Paulo, July 2010), and at international workshops on "Basic income and income redistribution" (University of Luxembourg, April 2011) and on "Anti-Poverty Programmes in a Global perspective" (Wissenschaftszentrum Berlin, June 2011).

[10] University of Louvain, Chaire Hoover d'éthique économique et sociale

[11] This is the definition adopted by the Basic Income Earth Network (BIEN), www.basicincome.org.

---

and because it prevents the income guarantee from creating an unemployment trap. And its being free of counterpart matters because of the bargaining power it affords to the weakest in their relationship with bosses, spouses and officials and the contribution thereby made, not just to their purchasing power but to the quality of the various dimensions of their lives.

Because of the combination of these features, a basic income has been advocated as the most emancipatory way of fighting unemployment without perpetuating poverty or of fighting poverty without generating unemployment. In connection with each of the features listed above, it has also been the subject of fierce criticisms from both the right and the left. In the present context, I shall make no attempt to give a general overview of the rich discussion triggered by these criticisms.[12] I shall focus instead on one dimension of this discussion that is gaining in importance every day. Most of the arguments about the (un)desirability and (un)feasibility of a basic income have been formulated within the framework of fairly self-contained nation-states. This may have made a lot of sense in the case of the brief British debate in the 1920s, in the case of the hardly less brief US debate in the late 1960s, perhaps even in the case of the European debates that started in the 1980s. But how could it possibly make any sense in the twenty first century, in the era of globalization, in an era in which capital and goods, people and ideas are crossing national borders as they have never done before? In this new context, are the prospects for a basic income not deeply altered. Indeed, have they not dramatically worsened?

---

[12] See e.g. Van Parijs (2006), Caputo ed. (2012), De Wispelaere & al. ed. (2012), and Van Parijs & Vanderborght (in progress) for general overviews; Van Parijs (1995), Van Donselaar (2009) and Birnbaum (2012) for extensive discussions of the ethical justification of the idea; and Standing (2011) for a demonstration of its contemporary relevance.

Does the European Social Model Have a Future?

# The challenge of migration:
# race to the bottom and ethnic diversity

Of the many aspects of globalization, trans-national migration is the one that creates the most obvious threat to the sustainability of a significant unconditional basic income. The existence of such a threat is particularly disturbing for many supporters of basic income. For the joint appeal of equality and freedom, which endeared basic income to them should also make them firm supporters of free migration. The real freedom to choose the way to spend one's life should encompass the freedom to choose where to spend it, and this freedom should not be restricted to those who happen to be born in the privileged part of the planet. Why is there a tension between trans-national migration and the sustainability of basic income schemes? For two reasons, one that is primarily economic, the other specifically political.[13]

The first reason has to do with the *race to the bottom* which trans-national migration, both effective and potential, is expected to trigger. The underlying mechanism has two components. One of these concerns the tax base required to fund a basic income and all other social transfers. Note, first of all, that even in the absence of any transnational migration of people, the trans-national mobility of capital already presents a threat, at least in combination with the trans-national mobility of products. If globalization means that capital can move freely from one country to another and be invested so as to produce goods that can in turn be exported freely from one country to another, profits will be hard to tax by any national government in a globalized economy. Significant redistribution remains possible, however, as long as the highly-skilled and hence highly paid workers are hardly mobile trans-nationally. But as soon as the trans-national mobility of human capital ceases to be marginal, genuine redistribution from people with a high labour income becomes problematic too.

---

[13] See Howard (2006) for a discussion of this issue in a broadly similar spirit, with a focus on the first dimension of the challenge.

To the extent that the welfare state conforms strictly to an insurance logic, it escapes such pressure. As it involves no genuine or ex-ante redistribution, the contributions paid out of wages are simply the counterpart of entitlements to earnings-related old-age pensions, short-term unemployment benefits and other forms of risk compensation. But many aspects of conventional welfare states do involve ex ante redistribution, typically when child benefits, old age pensions, sickness pay or unemployment benefits funded by proportional or progressive contributions are not actuarially equivalent to the contributions paid, but either fixed at the same level for everyone or not allowed to fall below some floor or to rise above some ceiling. Ex ante redistribution in this sense, i.e. redistribution that reaches beyond the ex-post redistribution inherent in any inherent scheme, is by no means restricted to benefits paid to the economically inactive. Ex ante redistribution from the better paid more productive workers to the less productive ones is also involved in in-work benefits such as wage subsidies or earned income tax credit. And it is blatantly present when the welfare state involves a general minimum income guarantee, whether or not it is means-tested and work-tested.[14]

It is those genuinely redistributive transfer schemes that are bound to be threatened if a significant part of the better paid workers, the net contributors to such schemes, seriously consider the possibility of moving to countries in which their skills could command a higher post-tax-and-transfer return. Once this is thought to be happening, firms will consider settling in places where, for a given cost, they can offer a higher take-home pay. Whether or not these workers and firms actually move, the fear that they might do will lead governments to reduce the rate of

---

[14] This distinction between sheer ex-post or insurance-based redistribution and ex-ante or genuine redistribution is orthogonal to the distinction between transfer schemes that involve ex-ante payments, i.e payments made without any prior control of the beneficiaries' incomes, and schemes that operate through ex-post payments, i.e. payments made selectively in the light of information about the beneficiaries' income over a given period. As it tends to be administered, a negative income tax scheme is ex ante in the first sense ex post in the latter, while a private pension scheme is merely ex post in the first sense and ex ante in the second sense.

taxation on high incomes and/or to tie the benefits more closely to the contributions paid, and thereby to reduce the level of genuine redistribution. Assuming it needs to be funded by taxation of some sort, an unconditional basic income is a paramount example of a genuinely redistributive scheme, and its prospects can therefore be expected to get worse as the growing mobility of net contributors triggers inter-national tax competition.

As if this were not bad enough, the race-to-the-bottom mechanism has a second component on the recipient side. Globalization involves not only increasing migration of the high earners, but also of the low earners and potential benefit claimants. In this context, countries with more generous benefit systems — in terms of levels and/or conditions — will operate as "welfare magnets". As suggested by the observation of inter-state migration in the United States, differences in generosity may have less impact by persuading some people to leave their country in order to move to another than by determining the destination of those who have decided to migrate.[15] This will again put pressure on any scheme that involves significant genuine redistribution, whether it takes the form of cash transfers, subsidized health care, subsidized education or wage subsidies. In order to stem the selective migration of likely net beneficiaries, countries with generous schemes will be under pressure to make them less generous. Downward social competition will thus join hands with downward tax competition.

This economically motivated race to the bottom is one mechanism through which trans-national migration (actual or merely potential) can be expected to worsen the prospects of a significant unconditional basic income, indeed even the prospects of maintaining the levels and the degrees of unconditionality of existing schemes. There is, however, a second, specifically political mechanism through which actual (unlike merely potential) migration makes genuine redistribution shakier. Immigration tends to make populations more heterogeneous in racial,

---

[15]  See, for example, Peterson & Rom (1990), Peterson (1995) and Borjas (1999) for discussions of this phenomenon in the case of the United States.

religious and linguistic terms, and this ethnic heterogeneity tends to weaken the political sustainability of a generous redistributive system through two distinct mechanisms.[16] Firstly, the degree of heterogeneity affects the extent to which the net contributors to the transfer system identify with (those they perceive as) its net beneficiaries, i.e. the extent to which they regard them as "their own people", to whom they owe solidarity. In particular, when genuinely redistributive schemes are perceived to benefit more than proportionally some ethnic groups, the resentment of those who fund them will tend to block the expansion of such schemes and even to jeopardize their viability. Secondly, institutionalized solidarity can also be expected to be weaker in a heterogeneous society because ethnic differences erect obstacles to smooth communication and mutual trust between the various components of the category that can expect to gain from generous redistributive schemes. Such obstacles make it more difficult for all net beneficiaries to coordinate, organize and struggle together.[17] As a result of the conjunction of these two mechanisms, one can expect institutionalized redistribution to be less generous in more heterogeneous societies than in more homogeneous ones, as seems confirmed by empirical evidence.[18] If globalization means a constant flow of migrants, therefore, it is not even necessary to appeal to a competitive race-to-the-bottom to diagnose gloomy prospects for a significant unconditional basic income in a globalized context. Growing ethnic diversity provides sufficient ground for pessimism⊠

Faced with this twofold challenge posed by trans-national migration, is there no better option than to mourn the epoch of tight borders, or perhaps to dream of a world freed of massive international inequalities and of the irresistible migration pressures they feed? Far from it. True, we must honestly recognize that generous solidarity is easier to imagine and implement in a closed homogeneous society cosily protected by robust borders against both opportunistic migration and

---

[16] See the essays collected in Van Parijs ed. (2003)

[17] For this sort of reason, Marx and Engels were hostile to the immigration of Irishmen into the industrial towns of the North of England (see Brown 1992).

[18] See e.g. Alesina & al. 2003, Desmet & al. 2005.

ethnic heterogeneity. But having done that, we must actively explore and advocate three possible responses to the challenge we face. Along the way we shall discover that, far from worsening them, some aspects of this challenge actually improve the prospects of transfer systems of the basic income type.

# A global basic income?

A first response that can be given to the first aspect of the challenge — the race to the bottom — is obvious enough. If nations are no longer able to perform their redistributive function because of their immersion in a global market, let us globalize redistribution. Globalized redistribution can of course hardly be expected to take the form of a complex, subtly structured welfare state that stipulates precisely what qualifies as a relevant need and the conditions under which, the way in which and the extent to which social solidarity will cover it. If it is ever to come into being, it will need to take the crude form of very simple benefits funded in a very simple way. Cultural heterogeneity being maximal at the world level, we cannot expect a sufficient consensus to arise on anything very detailed. But should this heterogeneity not also make us doubt that we shall ever get anything on that scale?

This skepticism is not shared by a number of people who have been arguing, sometimes with great persistence, for a universal basic income that would be truly universal. For example, the political philosopher Thomas Pogge (Yale University) has been arguing for a "global resources dividend", to be funded out of a tax on the use or sale of the natural resources of the earth (see Pogge 1994, 1995, 2002: ch.8). The underlying idea is that the populations of the countries that happen to shelter these resources have no sound ethical claim to the exclusive appropriation of their value, and that part of this value must enable the poor of the world to satisfy their basic needs. While noncommittal about the best way of achieving this objective, Pogge (2005) acknowledges that "something like a Global Basic Income may well be part of the best plan". Many others have come, often more explicitly, to a simple proposal of a universal basic income, usually inspired by the generous desire to substantially alleviate world poverty with a simple tool at a reasonable expense for the rich of the planet and/or by the need to make good use of the (supposedly) large revenues generated by taxes that may have a rationale of their own, typically the Tobin tax on international financial transactions.[19]

By far the most promising family of proposals along these lines, however, is rooted at the core of the climate change debate (see e.g. Busilacchi 2009). A growing consensus has emerged that the atmosphere of the earth has only a limited capacity to digest carbon emissions without triggering climatic phenomena that are most likely to be very damaging for significant and particularly vulnerable parts of the human population. As the causes of these phenomena are essentially of a global nature, global action is required and will be forthcoming with the appropriate speed and zeal only if all parties involved can view this collective action as a fair deal. But what counts as a fair deal? According to one interpretation, a fair deal means that those who are to benefit from the collective action — through the prevention of climate-related disasters such as floods or desertification — should contribute to its cost in proportion to the expected benefits. According to a second, less obnoxious interpretation, a fair deal is one that allocates the cost of the remedial action to be taken in proportion to the extent to which the consumption and production of each party to the deal contributed and is contributing to the harm to be remedied.

The most plausible interpretation, however, is neither in terms of co-operative justice (how should the cost of producing a public good be shared among those who benefit from it?) nor in terms of reparative

---

[19]  Thus, the Dutch artist Pieter Kooistra (1922-1998) set up a foundation under the name "UNO inkomen voor alle mensen" (A UN income for all people) in order to propagate his proposal of a small unconditional income for each human to be funded by issuing an ad hoc currency that cannot be hoarded (Kooistra 1983, 1994). In a more scholarly mode, the Canadian economist Myron Frankman (Mc Gill University), has been arguing for the feasibility of a "planet-wide citizen's income" funded by a worldwide progressive income tax (see Frankman 2002, 2004).

Does the European Social Model Have a Future?

justice (how should the costs that make up a public harm be shared among those who cause it?), but in terms of distributive justice: how is the value of scarce resources to be distributed among those entitled to them? More specifically, the carbon-absorbing capacity of the atmosphere is a natural resource to which all human beings have an equal claim. The best way of characterizing "climate justice" therefore consists in three steps. Firstly, determine, albeit approximately, the threshold which global carbon emissions should not exceed without creating serious damage. Secondly, sell to the highest bidders emission rights that amount in the aggregate, for a given period, to this threshold. The uniform equilibrium price determined through an auction of this type will trickle into the prices of all goods worldwide in proportion to their direct and indirect carbon content and accordingly affect consumption and production patterns in the broadest sense, including for example travelling and housing habits. Thirdly, distribute the (huge) revenues from such auction equally to all those with an equal right to make use of the "digestion power" of the atmosphere, i.e. to all members of mankind — rather than as an increasing function of current levels of carbon emission as in most of the tradable quota schemes discussed or implemented so far.[20]

If this is what a fair deal requires, a worldwide basic income is still not quite around the corner, but it is no longer a pipedream. No doubt, some implementation problems need to be solved. Distributing the proceeds to governments in proportion to their own estimates of the size of their population may look like a promising step forward, but it can be expected to trigger a backlash, owing to some governments and administrators misreporting the relevant data and not being above trying to seize much of the proceeds before they reach the population. More promising is a transnational scheme that involves a guarantee of reaching individuals, not just governments. To make it more manageable, one might think of restricting it initially to individuals above sixty or sixty five. In countries with a developed guaranteed pension system, the scheme could then

---

[20] See e.g. Glaeser (2011: 221) for a recent plea along these lines.

take the form of a modest "global" component in the benefit paid by the government to each elderly citizen. In countries with no such system, a new administrative machinery would have to be designed but, as the exemplary case of South Africa's guaranteed old-age pension demonstrates, the fact that transfers are concentrated on a subset of the population — and can therefore be higher per capita than if spread more thinly among people of all ages — means that delivery, security and monitoring costs can remain a fraction of the benefit paid out.[21]

Restricting the worldwide basic income, at least initially, to the elderly would have further advantages. By contributing to security in old age, it would foster the transition to lower birth rates in those countries in which that transition has not yet happened: the insurance motive for having children would be structurally weakened. Further, by making the aggregate benefit dependent on the number of people who reach an advanced age, it would provide governments of poorer countries with incentives to improve public health, education and other factors that contribute to longer life expectancy. And by being initially strongly biased in favour of richer countries in which life expectancy is far higher, it would increase the probability of being accepted while paving the way for a smooth increase of transfers from richer to poorer countries as the ratios of old to young gradually converge.

However, as a quick calculation shows (see Table 1), one has to be careful about the selection of the cut off age. If the proceeds of a carbon tax were shared in proportion to total population, the US and the EU would be big net contributors, China a moderate one, and Africa a big beneficiary. If the proceeds were shared in proportion to the population over 65, the net contributions of the US and China, as expected, would be perceptibly reduced, but the EU's net contribution would be turned into a net benefit, and Africa's net benefit into a net contribution. By the time the world is ripe for a scheme of this sort, African life expectancy might have caught up sufficiently. If not, 65 would not be the right cut-off age.

---

[21] See e.g. Case & Deaton 1998.

**Table 1 Shares of world population and carbon emissions**

|  | US | EU | CN | AF |
|---|---|---|---|---|
| Share of world carbon emissions | 20.0 | 13.7 | 21.5 | 3.6 |
| Share of world population | 4.7 | 7.4 | 19.7 | 14.8 |
| Share of world population 65+ | 7.6 | 16.3 | 20.9 | 0.4 |

Sources: www.wolframalpha.com + Wikipedia "List of countries by carbon dioxide emissions" (January 2010)

# A Euro-dividend ?

There are good reasons to believe that we currently lack the political structures and administrative capacity to implement anything like a worldwide basic income in the foreseeable future, whether or not it is age-specific, and whether it is funded by a carbon tax or through some other means. Hence the importance — both for their own sake and as preludes to worldwide schemes — of considering moves in this direction on a scale that is smaller, yet still large enough to incorporate many countries and thereby to counter the pressure of tax and social competition that hinders the capacity of each of them to carry out generous redistribution. One might imagine something of this sort emerging in the context of NAFTA or Mercosur.[22] However, because of the unprecedented process of supra-national institution-building which has gradually given it its present shape and because of the nature of the problems it now faces, the most interesting case is provided by the European Union.

Long before the current economic and political crisis, the single European market has been strengthening its grip on the margin of freedom enjoyed by the member state's distributive policies. This has helped feed the public opinion's hostility to the "neo-liberal" orientation

---

[22] Howard (2007) makes a plea for a basic income at the level of NAFTA.

of European integration and an urgent call for more "social Europe". More social Europe can mean more ambitious labour standards, or more investment in poor regions for the sake of social cohesion, or the adoption of targets for the employment of the less skilled. And in these various dimensions, it is already well on its way. As national transfer systems are coming under pressure, however, a more social Europe can also and arguably must mean a direct involvement of the EU in inter-personal transfers.⊠

This option is no longer an idle dream. It is one that cannot but come to the mind of anyone who tries to think seriously about why the Eurozone has been driven so quickly into an acute crisis by divergence in the competitiveness of member states no longer able to devalue their separate currencies, while the fifty Unites States, each similarly disabled, seem to cope happily with their single currency, despite divergences in competitiveness that can be no less dramatic than among European countries. As pointed out by both Paul Krugman and Joseph Stiglitz, the fundamental reason for this difference has to do with the operation, in the US, of two powerful stabilizers which are largely absent in the Eurozone: a high level of inter-state migration and a bulky redistributive tax-and-transfer system that operates overwhelmingly at the federal level. Because linguistic hurdles will make inter-country migration less frequent and costlier in the EU than in the US, the EU will have to count even more than the US on trans-national transfers that will buffer automatically any divergence, without any endless sequence of crisis meetings between governors or prime ministers, and thereby prevent ailing member states from being caught in a hopeless spiral of higher transfer liabilities and lower tax revenues.

How could the EU, or at least its Eurozone component, enter the highly sensitive business of inter-personal redistribution? There is no way in which one can expect it to develop, along US lines, a complex system of federal income taxation, old age pensions, health care insurance, earnings tax credit, food stamps and assistance to needy families. There will never be such an EU-wide (or even Eurozone-wide) mega-welfare state. Nor is there a need to supra-nationalize social insurance systems in the strict sense — as distinct from genuinely redistributive schemes: the pressure on them is sufficiently mild not to justify the development of an EU-wide system, even though increased trans-national worker mobility may foster convergence across member states and thereby further swell the sort of mobility that is precisely at the source of part of the problem. The most pressing need concerns the strictly redistributive aspects of the transfer system, in particular minimal income protection.

To address this need, Philippe Schmitter and Michael Bauer (2001) proposed the gradual introduction of an EU-wide *Eurostipendium* targeting the poorest European citizens. In their eyes, the many difficulties generated by the management of the EU's common agricultural policy and regional aid make a reallocation of funds devoted to income support in the European Union highly desirable. They suggest paying about 100 dollars per month to each European citizen whose income is below one third of the average income in the European Union, i.e. below about 450 dollars per month (EU15 in 2001).

This kind of scheme suffers from two obvious structural defects. Firstly, it involves a poverty trap at the individual level: citizens who earn just below one third of the average European income will receive a benefit of about 100 dollars, while those who earn slightly more will receive nothing, and thereby end up worse off than some of those earning less. Secondly, it involves what could be characterized as an inequality trap at the country level. To understand the nature of this trap, consider two countries with an identical average income. The one in which incomes are more unequally distributed will have a higher proportion of its population below the chosen threshold. However the scheme is funded, it will therefore benefit more from the proposed scheme (or contribute less to it) than the one with the more equal distribution. In addition, the implementation of such a scheme requires a homogeneous definition of the personal income to be taken into account for the sake of assessing whether some citizen's income falls below the threshold. What should be included in this income — home-grown food, home ownership, the earnings of one's co-habiting partner, etc. — or excluded from it — work-related expenses, alimonies, financial burden of dependent children, etc.

— and how intrusively income tests can or must be conducted are notoriously sensitive issues which are unlikely to find workable solutions at a supranational level.

An apparently more radical proposal is therefore far more realistic.[23] It consists in introducing a genuine unconditional basic income throughout the EU (or at least the Eurozone) at a level that could vary according to the average cost of living in each of the member states. This Euro-dividend could, for example, amount to 100 dollars net per month in the countries with the highest cost of living and be lower in others. With time, an upward convergence would gradually take place, as the levels of prices and incomes converge. Such a scheme has the advantage of requiring no means test, and hence no homogeneous definition and monitoring of relevant income. Moreover it gets rid in one swoop of both structural defects of Schmitter and Bauer's euro-stipendium. There is no risk for poor households to suffer a decrease in their net incomes as their earnings increase, since the latter are simply added to the Euro-dividend. Nor is there a risk for countries to be punished for adopting policies that reduce inequality and poverty (with a given average income), since the level of transnational transfer is not determined by the number of people that fall below the chosen threshold.

Like a worldwide basic income, such a Euro-dividend may need to be introduced in steps. Some have argued that one should start with farmers. By far the largest item in the budget of the European Union is the Common Agricultural Policy, which accounts for nearly half of the EU's expenditures. A shift from subsidizing the price of agricultural products to supporting the income of farmers has been advocated for a long time — and partly implemented — in order to avoid wasteful overproduction and unfair disparities.[24] The trouble for the sustainability of a systematic formula of this sort is that the category of "farmer" can

---

[23] See Van Parijs & Vanderborght (2001).

[24] This was already part of a plea for an EU-wide basic income by the British conservative member of the European Parliament Brandon Rhys-Williiams in 1975. See also Lavagne & Naud (1992).

easily become fuzzy, especially when a sizeable reward is attached to belonging to it. [25] Confining the payment to a particular age group may therefore again be the best option if one is to move gradually to a universal basic income. However, the European Union sees itself as having to address insufficient rather than excessive birth rates. Consequently, child benefits are a more attractive candidate than old-age pensions. Moreover, the fight against child poverty is regularly asserted as a top priority by all member states. An EU-wide universal child benefit may therefore constitute the best first step towards a genuine Euro-dividend?[26]

Whether reaching the whole population or restricted to children, a Euro-dividend needs to be funded. How? One could think of reassigning the agricultural expenditure and the so-called structural funds. But part of this expenditure arguably serves a valuable non-redistributive purpose, and even if the bulk of the corresponding revenues could be reallocated to the funding of a Euro-dividend for all European citizens, the level of the latter would have a hard time exceeding EUR 10 per month.[27]

A more plausible alternative that has been explored is a tax on the use of fossil energy.[28] Long before climate change became a major concern, such a tax had been proposed in response to both the need to slow down the depletion of valuable natural resources out of fairness to future generations and by the need to internalize the negative externalities closely associated with the use of fossil energy, such as atmospheric and

---

[25] To give an order of magnitude: The agricultural policy is costing about 50 billion EUR (46.7% of the total EU budget in 2006), i.e an average of about 5000 EUR annually (or 500 USD monthly) per full-time farmer. Source: Wikipedia "Budget of the European Union", 2006 figures (consulted January 2010).

[26] As proposed, for example, by Atkinson (1993).

[27] The agricultural expenditures of EUR 50 billion would amount to about EUR 100 per capita annually. This could reach EUR 160 if the 32 billion of structural funds could be added. (Source: Wikipedia "Budget of the European Union", 2006 figures, consulted January 2010). If restricted to children up to 15, the amounts would be about EUR 650 and EUR 1070 per annum, respectively.

[28] See e.g. see Genet & Van Parijs (1992), Davidson (1995).

acoustic pollution, traffic jams and the cluttering of public spaces. The case for a tax of this sort is of course further strengthened by the growing consensus regarding the greenhouse effects of the use of fossil energy. The metric of the tax base may vary somewhat depending on whether depletion, direct negative externalities or carbon emissions provide the rationale, but the recommended level of tax should exceed significantly the competitive value of the volume of emission permits that derive from global climate considerations, as discussed above in connection with the idea of a global basic income.[29]

It is of course a necessary feature of a basic income funded in this way that it should be redistributing from countries with a high consumption of fossil energy to countries with a low consumption. This is not problematic if differences in energy consumption are essentially determined by differences in wealth — which is massively the case across regions of the world, but less so across member states of the European Union. Nor is it problematic if differences are essentially determined by the extent to which the various countries adopt effective energy-saving strategies: this is how appropriate incentives are supposed to work. However, a country's level of energy consumption is also affected by some of its natural feature, in particular how cold its climate happens to be. One might want to argue that the populations of colder countries have to pay the fair price of their choice of remaining in an environment where living is costlier — just as the true cost of living in a sprawling suburban habitat needs to be borne by those who opt for it rather than for a more concentrated urban life. But those populations may understandably feel that it would be unfair to make them pay a heavy price for wanting to live where their ancestors did and oppose staunch resistance to using a high energy tax for the purposes of trans-national redistribution.

---

[29] For example, by extrapolating some earlier estimates (Genet & Van Parijs 1992), one can expect a tax corresponding to reasonable assessments of the negative externalities associated with the use of fossil energy to yield a monthly revenue of slightly above EUR 100 per capita at the European level.

Should one then go for personal income taxation as the main source of funding of a Euro-dividend? Just as the income to be taken into account for means-tested benefits, the definition of taxable personal income is extremely sensitive politically. What expenses can be deducted from earnings? How does the composition of the household affect the amount of personal income that is taxable? How are home ownership and mortgages being taken into account? And so on. Personal income taxes, like means-tested benefits, therefore, are likely to remain a national or even sub-national prerogative.

At the European level, there is, however, a far more straightforward alternative: the Value Added Tax, an indirect tax paid by the consumer in proportion to the value added to the product purchased at every stage in its production. This tax has also been proposed at the national level as the most appropriate way of financing a basic income in various countries.[30] Whether in developed or in less developed countries, the main advantages claimed for VAT over the income tax at the national level are that it has a tax base that extends more widely beyond wages and that it turns out to be, if anything, less regressive than actual income tax schemes, adulterated as these tend to be by exemptions, discounts, the separate taxation of capital income, loopholes and sheer evasion. This argument is also relevant at the European level. But at that level, VAT funding has further advantages over income tax funding. Unlike the definition of personal income, the definition of value added for tax purposes is already homogenized at EU level, VAT is already used to fund part of the EU budget, and the fixing of rates by each member state is strongly constrained by EU legislation. The Value Added Tax, possibly supplemented by a modest EU-level energy tax, is therefore by far the most promising avenue for funding a significant Euro-dividend, and by extension any other significant supra-national basic income.[31]

---

[30] For example by Roland Duchatelet (1992) for Belgium, by Pieter Leroux (2006) for South Africa and by Götz Werner (2007) for Germany.

[31] As came up in the US debate on the "fair tax" proposal, a very modest basic income — for example, the "prebate" advocated by Mike Huckabee, a candidate at the 2008

---

Whether funded in this or in practically any other way, a Euro-dividend, just as any other supra-national basic income, would operate a systematic redistribution of wealth from the richer to the poorer parts of the territory concerned, and from the metropolitan to the rural areas. It would thereby help stabilize the population and avoid some of the undesirable externalities of migration. At the same time, it would buffer automatically, without needing ad hoc decisions, any asymmetric shock or productivity divergence affecting the various member states of the Eurozone. Unlike other conceivable supra-national schemes, it would create no perverse incentives on the individual or national level. Nor would it disrupt, homogenize or undermine current national welfare systems. Quite to the contrary. By fitting a modest yet firm base under the existing, more finely calibrated national redistribution institutions, it would help strengthen them and stabilize their diversity.

## National basic incomes in a global economy ?

The Euro-dividend was discussed here as a not too fanciful example of how a basic income could be implemented at a level that is higher than that of individual nation-states, while still falling far short of the world scale. The advantage it possesses over country-level redistributive schemes is that it is less vulnerable to tax and social competition and hence can be said to address the first of the two challenges that stem from globalization. But compared to these less global schemes, it has the

---

Republican presidential primary — is a natural correlate of any value added tax or consumption tax levied for whatever purpose. It provides the exact analogue to exempting the slices of income below the poverty threshold from direct taxation: it guarantees that those who are already poor without being taxed are not made even poorer by the tax. Suppose, for example, that the rate of VAT is 20% and that the poverty threshold is fixed at 600 dollars per person per month, taking the impact of the tax on prices into account. To guarantee that no poor person is a net contributor, the basic income needs to be fixed at a level at least equal to the poverty threshold multiplied by the rate of VAT, in this example 600 dollars x 20/100 = 120 dollars per month.

disadvantage of faring worse as regards the second challenge: it operates at a level that involves a larger and above all more heterogeneous population, with a weaker common identity, a weaker sense of belonging to the same political community, a weaker set of political institutions and a plurality of distinct public opinions and public debates separated by the use of distinct languages.

As regards a politically sustainable generous basic income, therefore, we may have to keep pitching our hopes at the level of national or even sub-national entities. After the exploration of a global basic income and of the Euro-dividend as an example of a regional basic income, we now turn to the third possible response to our initial challenge. Admittedly, greater homogeneity comes at the cost of greater vulnerability to "opportunistic" behaviour by both net contributors and net beneficiaries. Such vulnerability to social and tax competition will be reduced when the geographically more limited schemes will be able to operate against the background of a geographically broader redistributive system. When firms and people are trans-nationally mobile, countries will tend to reduce the degree of redistribution in order to attract or keep taxpayers and businesses or in order to dissuade social benefit claimants. But if, owing to the existence of some supranational redistributive scheme, the former contribute to some extent and the latter benefit to some extent whether in or out of the country concerned, reducing the degree of intra-national redistribution will be a less compelling option, and the race to the bottom will be largely neutralized. However, as long as trans-national redistribution across relevant countries is weak or inexistent, generous national redistribution will remain highly vulnerable in a world characterized by high and increasing trans-national mobility.

How can this vulnerability be reduced? Firstly, by maintaining or strengthening linguistic and cultural obstacles to migration. If the language spoken in each country is different from the language spoken in any other and difficult to learn by non-native speakers, if the associated cultures are distinctive and hard to integrate into, generous solidarity would be sustainable in all of them even in the absence of any administrative obstacle to migration: both potential beneficiaries and current contributors would balk at the prospect of heavy investment in language learning and cultural adjustment. These linguistic obstacles tend to shrink, however. As regards, firstly, the migration of potential beneficiaries, they are being eroded by the growth of diasporas that retain their original language and hence provide micro-environments into which newcomers can smoothly integrate. At the same time, the linguistic obstacles to the migration of potential contributors are being eroded by the spreading of English as a lingua franca, which makes it less burdensome, both domestically and professionally, to settle abroad, especially but not only in the English-speaking parts of the world. Nonetheless, as long as they exist, these linguistic differences and the associated cultural differences will remain a major brake on transnational migration, and there are good — though by no means obvious — grounds for wanting at least some of them to persist.[32]

Can one think of any other forms of protection against the race to the bottom? Definitely. But they are of an altogether different nature, depending on whether one is concerned with undesirable entries or with undesirable exits. Administrative obstacles to the entry of potential beneficiaries have been advocated and used to protect small-scale redistributive schemes ever since they existed. Thus, in the very first treatise on social assistance, Johannes Ludovicus Vives (1526), recommended that each municipality should look only after its own poor. As to those coming from elsewhere, they should be given "a modest viaticum" and, unless they are coming from a region at war, be sent them back home. Two and a half centuries later, Adam Smith (1776: ch.10) referred to a milder version of this protective strategy: an English rule to the effect that an "undisturbed residence" of forty days is required before poor people can belong to the "own poor" for whom each parish has to provide. And when Governor Cristovam Buarque introduced a guaranteed minimum income for families in the Federal District of Brasilia in the mid-1990s, a residence period of ten years was imposed before newcomers from other parts of Brazil could claim the benefits.

---

[32]  See Van Parijs (2011, chapter 5).

---

Similarly, Brazil's 2004 "citizenship income law" restricts entitlement, among non-Brazilians, to people who have been living in Brazil for at least five years.

There are two problems with protective strategies of this sort. One is that the restriction may be struck down on grounds of discrimination. This can be discrimination between citizens of the same country when the basic income is introduced at a sub-national level. For example, the first version of the Alaska dividend scheme differentiated the amount to which a resident was entitled according to the length of residence in the state. The US Supreme Court decided that this violated the principle of equality between all US citizens. This is why the final version of the dividend took the form of a straight universal basic income.[33] Even when the basic income is introduced at a national level, the discriminatory character of the residence requirement may be a problem if national legislation is constrained by supra-national rules, as is the case, in particular, in the European Union.

If the basic income were introduced in the EU as a whole, however, or at the level of the US or indeed of any sovereign state not incorporated into a wider entity that imposes non-discrimination among all its members, residence requirements would in principle be conceivable, and indeed they are routinely used to protect existing conditional minimum income guarantees. However, as regards a universal basic income, they face a second difficulty which arises irrespective of the scale at which the scheme is being introduced. The difference with benefits that target the economically inactive is that a basic income — just as a negative income tax — also benefits workers. The residence requirement would typically mean that, though taxed from the first dollar earned at the high rate required to fund a basic income for all long-term residents, the workers who do not satisfy the residence requirement would not receive the basic income (or uniform tax credit) to which all other workers are entitled. If administered in the form of a refundable tax credit, this would have the

---

[33]  See e.g. Hammond (1994).

bizarre consequence that the take-home pay of workers would differ significantly depending on how long they have been residing in the relevant entity. And however it is administered it would involve a major distortion at the lower end of the labour market, with some able to turn down lousy jobs thanks to their entitlement to an unconditional basic income and others forced to pick them up in the absence of this fall-back option.

The alternative to the residence requirement is of course the more radical option recommended by Vives to 16th century municipalities: the denial of entry to those likely to be net beneficiaries of the basic income scheme. For sub-national schemes or national schemes for member states of the European Union, this is even more difficult to conceive than discriminatory access to social benefits because of free movement within the boundaries of the entity of which one is a citizen being regarded as a fundamental right. For unconstrained states and for the EU as a whole, however, this is the standard strategy in place. It faces neither of the two difficulties that plague the residence requirement. But it is weakened by the unavoidability of illegal immigration and subsequent regularization. And above all, it crudely exposes the cruel dilemma between sustainable generosity towards the weakest among one's own citizens and generous hospitality to anyone who wishes to come in. This dilemma is the most painful challenge for the Left throughout the more developed world. It is inescapable in a deeply unequal world and holds for any form of genuine — i.e. not merely insurance-based — redistribution, but most blatantly for a universal basic income. The ultimate aim is global distributive justice. But the safest way to approach it is not to let existing redistributive systems be destroyed by open and non-discriminatory borders. Comparatively generous institutionalized solidarity needs protection against unsustainable immigration by likely beneficiaries. Its survival and its spreading are needed on the way to its globalization.

To ensure the survival of generous redistribution, protection is required not only against undesirable entries — the immigration of likely beneficiaries —, but also against undesirable exits — the emigration of actual contributors. As regards the latter, administrative protection of the sort discussed in connection with the former — residence requirements and filtering at the borders — are of precious little help. Is there anything else at our disposal? Only something of an altogether different kind: some territorial, non-ethnic patriotism, i.e. some sort of attachment to a place, some sort of allegiance or fidelity to the political community it hosts and the solidarity it achieves, that makes high-earners wish to live, work, contribute there, rather than shop around for the highest return to their human capital.[34] Of course this attitude may tend to be harder to sustain as the community becomes both less distinctive (externally) and more heterogeneous (internally) as a result of globalization and migration. But when combined with the preservation of language borders and administrative buffers against the immigration of potential net beneficiaries, it may suffice in many cases to prevent a comparatively generous single-country basic income from falling prey to the race to the bottom.

What about the second aspect of the challenge of migration: the growing heterogeneity that increasingly characterizes most countries in the world, despite linguistic and administrative hurdles? When the immigrant population accounts for a significant proportion of the population, its adequate integration into the host society is important in order for generous solidarity to be sustainable, both politically — by avoiding the erosion of feelings of solidarity embracing the whole population — and financially – by avoiding the swelling and perpetuation, from one generation to the next one, of vast pockets of people who are difficult to incorporate into the productive system. Is the very unconditionality of a basic income not a major disadvantage in this context, precisely because it does nothing to foster a quick integration of ethnic minorities through work?

It is important to note, firstly, that although a basic income would do worse, in this respect, than more coercive workfare-type policies, it

---

[34] See Steiner (2003) for a critique of this "solidaristic patriotism", and Van Parijs (2003: 209-212) for a response.

would do better than means-tested schemes that create dependency traps. Secondly, especially when inadequate competence in the language of the host country and the associated hardening of residential and educational ghettos risk creating a vicious circle of exclusion, it is worth considering the option of connecting the right to benefits to the duty to attend suitable language courses which the government would have the responsibility to provide. Thirdly, the need to preserve or create a sense of national identity in the face of ethnic heterogeneity may require and justify not only an inclusive national rhetoric that values cultural diversity, but also specific policies, such as an intelligently designed compulsory civil service or other ways of spreading across all ethnic groups a common ethos of contribution to the common good.

This sequence of considerations is indispensable to indicate why and under what conditions basic income proposals can keep making realistic sense at the national level even in the era of globalization. Yet, the best proof of a possibility remains a reality. Before concluding, it is therefore worth mentioning that the only case of a genuine basic income introduced at a sub-national level is still alive and healthy after thirty years, and that for the first time in history a basic income has been introduced at the national level in a country which would not have a priori seemed an obvious candidate for such an experiment. The sub-country in which a basic income was introduced in 1982 is of course the state of Alaska. For three decades, the Alaska Permanent Fund has been collecting part of Alaska's oil revenues, investing them in stocks worldwide and paying out once a year to all Alaskan residents a uniform dividend the level of which varies with the performance of the Permanent fund in the previous five years. In 2011, the amount was close to 1200 dollars and was paid to nearly 650.000 people.[35]

The surprise, however, came from Iran. In January 2010, the Iranian parliament approved by a narrow majority the so-called "targeted subsidy law", which combines three measures. Firstly, it scraps a large and

---

[35]  See Howard & Widerquist eds. (2012)

economically perverse implicit subsidy to oil consumption by both Iranian households and firms. It does so by bringing the comparatively very low domestic price of oil gradually in line with the international price. It uses 20 to 30% of the new revenues to subsidize directly producers hit by the price increase. Thirdly, it uses the bulk of the revenues to compensate the impact of the general price increase on the standard of living of the population by introducing a monthly cash subsidy for over 70 million Iranian citizens. This cash payment was expected to reach initially about 20 dollars per person per month and to gradually rise to 60 dollars. The rich, who consume directly and indirectly more oil than average would not be fully compensated for the price increase, but the poor would automatically be more than compensated. The first phase of the law came into effect in October 2010. It amounts to granting a small but genuine equal basic income to every citizen, with two major qualifications: the payment for all members of each household is made to its official head, i.e. mostly to men, and non-Iranian residents, mostly Iraqian and Afghan refugees, are not entitled to the grant.[36] Despite these shortcomings, the Iranian model may provide inspiration for other countries. Wherever one is seeking a "sustainable new deal" that combines ecological and social concerns, whether or not the country is resource-rich, making resource consumption more expensive and distributing the corresponding additional revenues equally to all is an obvious option to consider.[37]

---

[36] See esp. Tabatabai (2011). The government announced in January 2012 that, in the second phase of the programme, it intends to increase the amount of the uniform grant to most households, while inviting the 14% wealthiest households to waive their entitlement to the grant on a voluntary basis.

[37] In 2011, the Mongolian government also indicated that it would use part of the proceeds of its mineral resources to fund a regular basic income to its whole population: see http://binews.org/2011/09/mongolia-government-takes-steps-toward-implementing-an-alaskan-style-big/.

---

# Conclusion

In order to move forward under current circumstances, one can and must tread several paths simultaneously. Every opportunity must be seized to move towards something that starts resembling a worldwide basic income, most promisingly in the context of groping for a fair deal on global warming. Every opportunity must be seized to move towards something that starts resembling a supra-national, though still geographically limited, basic income, most promisingly at the level of the European Union. And wherever sufficient leeway has been kept at the national level, there is also ample room — as argued here — and many good reasons — as argued elsewhere[38] — to reform existing welfare states so that they incorporate at their very core a universal and unconditional individual basic income.

---

[38] See, for example, Van Parijs (2006) and, at greater length, Van Parijs & Vanderborght (in progress).

# References

Alesina, Alberto, Arnaud Devleeschauwer, William Easterly, Sergio Kurlat, Romain Wacziarg. 2003. "Fractionalization", *Journal of Economic Growth*, 8, 155-94.

Atkinson, Anthony B. 1993. "Beveridge, the National Minimum, and its future in a European context", STICERD Working Paper WSP/85, January 1993.

Birnbaum, Simon. 2012. *Basic Income Reconsidered: Social Justice, Liberalism and the Demands of Equality*, New York : Palgrave Macmillan.

Borjas, George J. 1999. "Immigration and Welfare Magnets", in *Journal of Labor Economics* 17(4), 607-37.

Brown, Christopher. 1992. "Marxism and the Transnational Migration of People", in *Free Movement* (B. Barry & R.E. Goodin eds.), Hemel Hempstead: Harvester, 127-44.

Busilacchi, Gianluca. 2009. Dagli rifiuti puó nascere un fiore: un reddito di base per salvare il pianeta", in *Reddito per tutti. Un'utopia concreta per l'era globale* (BIN Italia ed.), Roma: Manifestolibri, 167-176.

Caputo, Richard K. ed. 2012. *Basic Income Guarantee and Politics: International Experiences and Perspectives on the Viability of Income Guarantees*, New York : Palgrave Macmillan.

Case, Anne & Deaton, Angus. 1998. "Large cash transfers to the elderly in South Africa", *The Economic Journal* 108, 1330-61,

Davidson, Marc. 1995. "Liberale grondrechten en milieu. Het recht op milieugebruiksruimte als grondslag van een basisinkomen", in *Milieu* 5, 1995, 246-249.

Desmet, Klaus, Ignacio Ortuño-Ortín & Shlomo Weber. 2005. *Peripheral linguistic diversity and redistribution*. Université catholique de Louvain: CORE Discussion Paper 2005044.

Duchatelet, Roland. 1994. "An economic model for Europe based on consumption financing on the tax side and the basic income principle on the redistribution side", paper presented at the 5th BIEN Congress (London, September 8–10, 1994), 7 p.

Frankman, Myron J. *World Democratic Federalism: Peace and Justice Indivisible*. Houndmills, Basingstoke & New York: Palgrave-Macmillan, 2004.

Frankman, Myron J. 1998. "Planet-Wide Citizen's Income: Antidote to Global Apartheid, *Labour, Capital and Society* 31, 166-78.

Gantelet, Gilles & Maréchal, Jean-Paul eds. *Garantir le revenu: une des solutions a l'exclusion*, Paris: Transversales Science Culture, Document no. 3, mai 1992.

Genet, Michel & Van Parijs, Philippe. 1992. "Eurogrant", *Basic Income Research Group Bulletin* 15, 4-7.

Glaeser, Edward. 2011. *The Triumph of the City*. New York: Penguin 2011.

Hammond, Jay. 1994. *Tales of Alaska's Bush Rat Governor*, Alaska: Epicenter Press.

Howard. Michael W. 2006. "Basic Income and Migration Policy: A Moral Dilemma?", *Basic Income Studies* 1(1), Article 4.

Howard. Michael W. & Widerquist, Karl, eds. 2012. *Alaska's Permanent Fund Dividend: Examining its Suitability as a Model*, London: Palgrave-MacMillan.

Howard. Michael W. 2007. "A NAFTA Dividend: A Guaranteed Minimum Income for North America", *Basic Income Studies* 2(1), Article 1.

Kooistra, Pieter. 1983. *Voor*. Amsterdam: Stichting UNO-inkomen voor alle mensen.

Kooistra, Pieter. 1994. *Het ideale eigenbelang, Een UNO–Marshallplan voor alle mensen*, Kampen: Kok Agora.

Lavagne, Pierre & Naud, Frédéric. 1992 "Revenu d'existence: une solution à la crise agricole", in *Garantir le revenu: une des solutions a l'exclusion* (G. Gantelet & J.P. Maréchal eds.), Paris: Transversales, 1992, 95-106.

Leroux Pieter. 2006. *"Why a Universal Income Grant in South Africa should be financed through VAT and other Indirect Taxes"*, University of the Western Cape: School of Government.

Peterson, Paul E. & Rom, Mark C. 1990. *Welfare Magnets: A New Case for National Standards*, Washington (DC): Brookings.

Peterson, Paul E. 1995. *The Price of Federalism*, Washington (DC): Brookings.

Pogge, Thomas. 1994. "An Egalitarian Law of Peoples", *Philosophy and Public Affairs* 23, 195-224.

Pogge, Thomas. 1995. "Eine globale Rohstoffdividende", *Analyse und Kritik* 17, 183-208.

Pogge, Thomas. 2002. *World Poverty and Human Rights*. Cambridge : Polity Press.

Pogge. Thomas. 2005. "Global Justice as Moral Issue", interview with Alessandro Pinzani, *ethics@* 4(1), 1-6.

Schmitter, Philippe & Michael W. Bauer. 2001. "A (modest) proposal for expanding social citizenship in the European Union", *Journal of European Social Policy* 11 (1), 55-65.

Smith, Adam. 1776. *The Wealth of Nations*. Harmondsworth: Penguin Books, 1977.

Standing, Guy. 2011. *The Precariat: the New Dangerous Class*. London: Bloomsbury.

Steiner, Hillel. 2003. "Compatriot Solidarity and Justice among Thieves", in *Real Libertarianism Assessed: Political Theory after Van Parijs* (A. Reeve and A. Williams eds.), Basingstoke: Palgrave Macmillan, 161–71.

Tabatabai, Hamid. 2011. « The Basic Income Road to Reforming Iran's Price Subsidies », *Basic Income Studies* 6(1).

Van Donselaar, Gijs. 2009. *The Right to Exploit. Parasitism, Scarcity, and Basic Income*, Oxford: Oxford University Press.

Van Parijs, Philippe & Yannick Vanderborght. 2001. "From Euro-Stipendium to Euro-Dividend", *Journal of European Social Policy* 11, 342-346.

Van Parijs, Philippe 2003, "Hybrid Justice, Patriotism and Democracy: A Selective Reply", in *Real Libertarianism Assessed: Political Theory after Van Parijs* (A. Reeve and A. Williams eds.), Basingstoke: Palgrave Macmillan, 201–16.

Van Parijs, Philippe. 2006. "Basic Income: A simple and Powerful Idea for the Twenty First Century", in *Redesigning Distribution: Basic Income and Stakeholder Grants as Cornerstones of a More Egalitarian Capitalism* (E.O. Wright ed.), London & New York: Verso, 3-42.

Van Parijs, Philippe ed. 2003. *Cultural Diversity versus Economic Solidarity*, Brussels : De Boeck Université. Downloadable from http://www.uclouvain.be/en-12569.html.

Van Parijs, Philippe. *Linguistic Justice for Europe and for the World.* Oxford: Oxford University Press, 2011.

Van Parijs, Philippe & Yannick Vanderborght. *A Basic Income for All*, Cambridge: Harvard University Press, in progress. Expanded English edition of *L'Allocation universelle*. Paris: La Découverte, 2005. (German edition: Campus, 2005; Italian edition: Bocconi University Press, 2006; Spanish edition: Paidos, 2006; Portuguese edition: Civilizaçao Brasileira, 2006).

Vives, Johannes Ludovicus. 1526. *De Subventione Pauperum*, French translation: *De l'Assistance aux pauvres*, Brussels: Valero & fils, 1943.

Werner, Götz. 2007. *Einkommen für alle*, Köln : Kiepenheuer & Witsch.

Widerquist, Karl, José Antonio Noguera, Yannick Vanderborght & Jurgen De Wispelaere, eds. 2012. *Basic Income : An Anthology of Contemporary Research*, Oxford : Blackwell.

# 4

## *After Beveridge: towards a new settlement – radical change for the common good*

### *Anna Coote*

## Introduction

In these crisis-ridden times, there is a prevailing sense of turbulence and insecurity. We can respond by withdrawing into whatever we can find by way of self-protection. Or we can seize the moment to promote radical change for the common good.

The challenge is substantial. There were already profound inequalities in our societies when the global economy began to implode in 2008. Since then we have plunged into a new age of austerity with swingeing cuts in services and grants for health and social care, children and young people, homeless families, as well as third-sector programmes aimed at helping poor and vulnerable groups. These cuts will widen inequalities still further. Indeed, we have probably reached the end of the post war settlement, founded on the ideals of William Beveridge. Under this settlement, our governments were committed to raising taxes to build a framework of public goods and services that enabled everyone, on the basis of need rather than ability to pay, to be protected against the risks of illness and unemployment, to be decently educated and housed, and to have enough money to live on (Timmins, 2001). If the Beveridge era is at an end, what happens next?

We must find ways to move from where we are, with widening inequalities, accelerating climate change, depleting natural resources and a deepening slump in the global economy, to where most of us would want to be – living in a strong, healthy and just society, with a flourishing economy that respects the limits of the natural environment and with the capacity to leave a secure legacy for future generations.

This implies a major transition to an economy that serves the interests of people and the planet, rather than the other way around (Spratt et al., 2010), which in turn implies a repositioning of political goals, so that the pursuit of growth cedes precedence to the pursuit of well-being for all. Here I take 'well-being' to mean feeling good physically and mentally and being able to function in the world: it describes people's emotions, their sense of competence and connection to others (Bok, 2010; Michaelson et al., 2009). Crucially, the words 'for all' sum up an imperative to create conditions for everyone to enjoy well-being, regardless of background or circumstances. This calls for an equality of opportunity that is profound rather than shallow – depending not only on rules against unfair discrimination, but also on proactive fairness and 'sustainable social justice', meaning the fair and equitable distribution of social, environmental and economic resources between people, places and generations (Coote and Franklin, 2009).

The goal, then, is to move towards a new settlement, building on Beveridge but also incorporating new objectives to suit the conditions of the 21st century. It's a big agenda and I cannot hope to do justice to it all in this paper. I will first consider some of the problems inherent in the post-war settlement. Then I will focus on three important components of a new settlement, which are inter-related: growing the core economy and promoting co-production; redistributing paid and unpaid time; and moving from cure to prevention in order to address the underlying determinants of sustainable social justice. I conclude with a brief discussion of the conditions for radical change.

# Problems with the post-war settlement

Notwithstanding its immense achievements, the post-war settlement is due for an overhaul. From the outset, it has rested on the premise that the economy will continue to grow, yielding more taxes to pay for more and better services. There are two problems with this assumption. First, a return to economic growth is not only uncertain because of the nature of the global crisis, but also unsustainable, because even if the economy did grow, it could not be rendered 'weightless' in time to avert catastrophic damage to the natural environment (Jackson, 2009).

Second, there is little evidence that more of the same kind of public services would bring commensurate benefits. A defining characteristic of the post-war settlement has been that paid public servants provide help to individuals who are needy and have problems. It has saved a lot of people from destitution and early death, but it has evolved into a deficit model that generates a culture of atomised individualism and dependency. If you are just a passive recipient of the ministrations of others who are paid to look after you, you can lose control over what happens to you. If your voice is unheard and you feel unvalued, this undermines your physical and mental well-being. You get used to thinking that others know more and are better placed to fix your problems – although what they do may not deliver the best outcomes, because your own wisdom and capabilities have not been brought into play. In many services, especially health, you are treated as an individual (if you are lucky) or as a body part (if you are not), with no account taken of context or relationships.

By and large, our governments have responded to the economic crisis by trying to shift responsibility from the state to individuals and from public services to groups and organisations in commercial and non-profit sectors. This approach implies a massive shift from social solidarity to private arrangements, and from paid to unpaid labour. It pays no attention to forces within modern capitalism that lead to accumulations of wealth and power in the hands of a few at the expense of others, selectively restricting the ability of citizens to participate and benefit. It is likely to leave the poorest and least powerful a long way behind (Coote, 2010).

As with the post-war settlement, the response of our governments to the economic crisis is anchored in the politics of economic growth. Accordingly, the primary measure of success is Gross Domestic Product, on the manifestly false assumption that, while GDP is growing, increased wealth will 'trickle down' to make everyone richer and happier.

Can we build a new settlement that is fit for the twenty-first century? What resources and mechanisms are required? In the first place, we cannot rely on continuing economic growth, for reasons I have indicated. Without growth, we must get used to looking after ourselves and each other in much tighter fiscal conditions. Even with more progressive tax systems and more expansionary economic policies, we would still have to make every pound or euro stretch further. However, that should not lead inexorably to decline, because the conventional market economy is not the only resource available.

# Growing the core economy

There is potential for growth in what has been described as the 'core' economy: the human resources that comprise and sustain social life (Goodwin, 2003). These resources are embedded in the everyday lives of every individual (time, wisdom, experience, energy, knowledge, skills) and in the relationships among them (love, empathy, responsibility, caring, reciprocity, teaching, and learning). They are 'core' because they are central and essential to society. They have value and are exchanged. Yet they are largely uncommodified, un-priced, and unpaid, routinely ignored and often exploited. They underpin the market economy by raising children, caring for people who are ill, frail, and disabled, feeding families, maintaining households, and building and sustaining intimacies, friendships, social networks, and civil society. They have a key role, too, in safeguarding the natural economy, since everyday human behaviours and lifestyles strongly influence the way we use environmental resources.

The core economy, which involves the production and distribution of these vital human resources, can flourish and expand, or weaken and decline, depending on the circumstances and conditions within which it operates. It can 'grow' if it is recognised, valued, nurtured, and supported.

While the core economy is rooted in families and households, it extends well beyond the domestic sphere, operating through extended families, wider social networks, neighbourhoods, and communities of interest and place. It includes all the un-priced and unpaid activities that are carried out by friends looking out for one another, grandparents sharing childcare and helping out, parents being school governors, volunteers cleaning up local parks or visiting people who are housebound, neighbours doing each other's shopping or keeping each other's keys, or exchanging gossip and advice. It provides the essential social functions that keep people connected with one another. Some of these activities are formally organised – for example, through national charities or local authorities. Most arise organically from close social relationships. They are predominantly female activities: indeed, the fact that the core economy is distinct from the market economy both expresses and reinforces the historically gendered division of paid and unpaid labour.

The core economy underpins and gives shape to social and economic life. If people's everyday resources and relationships are brought into the centre of policy-making, strengthened and enabled to flourish, it becomes possible to move from an economy based on scarcity of economic resources to an economy based on abundance of human assets. It also becomes possible to move beyond a deficit model of need which focuses on problems that require fixing, to a more rounded and positive approach to promoting well-being. Co-production illustrates the point.

*Promoting co-production*

Co-production is a term used to describe a particular way of getting things done, where the people who are currently known as 'providers' and 'users' work together in an equal and reciprocal partnership, pooling different kinds of knowledge and skill. It draws upon a long history of self-help, mutual aid, asset-based community development and other forms of participative local action, including time banking; it adds up to much more than consultation or 'user' involvement (Cahn, 2001; Parks et al., 1981; Wann, 1995). It starts from the premise that people have assets not just problems and that everyone has something of value to contribute. Individuals play an active role, often alongside family members, neighbours, professionals, or others with a relevant interest, in deciding how they want to live and what it would take to improve their lives, and then play a significant part in realising their goals.

This way, co-production taps into the abundance of human resources in the core economy and encourages people to join forces and make common cause. There are countless examples of co-production in practice, ranging across health and social care, parenting, education, criminal justice and local authority decision-making (Slay and Robinson, 2011). At best, it builds local networks and strengthens the capacity of local groups; it changes the way people think about themselves and what they are capable of doing; it draws upon the direct wisdom and experience they have about what they need and what they can contribute. All these factors can help to improve well-being and prevent problems occurring or intensifying. By transforming the way people think about and act upon 'needs' and 'services', co-production has the potential to democratise the character and substance of the public realm. Equally, it can transform the way independent non-profit and commercial organisations do their work. It has strong implications for professionals and others who provide services, because they will have to change how they think about themselves, how they understand others and how they operate on a day-to-day basis. They must learn to work *with* people, rather than doing things *to* or *for* them (Boyle and Harris, 2009; Boyle et al., 2009, 2010).

But lest we get too starry-eyed about co-production, it is important to note that it is not a blue-print that can be applied in any circumstances to achieve pre-determined effects. It is a broad approach, based on a set of principles that may or may not be followed; the quality of outcomes will depend on who's involved, how and under what conditions. The problems discussed below apply in equal measure to the prospect of 'growing the core economy' and promoting co-production.

*Problems with the core economy and co-production*
The core economy does not float freely beyond the reach of public life and paid employment. Nor is it inherently good or right. It is profoundly influenced by the rules, protocols, and power relations that emanate from the state and the market. It shapes and sustains social and economic life. It also reflects and reproduces social and economic divisions and inequalities.

As I have noted, most of its transactions involve women working without wages – a pattern that generates lasting inequalities in job opportunities, income and power between women and men. These are often compounded by age, race, ethnicity, and disability.

Time is a key resource in the core economy. Everyone has the same amount of time but some people have a lot more control over how they use their time than others. Some people – mainly women – have low-paid jobs as well as heavy caring responsibilities, so they are poor in terms of time as well as income. Notably, around half of lone parents can't earn enough money to stay out of poverty while making sure their children are looked after (by themselves or someone else), however long or hard they work (Burchardt, 2008). How paid and unpaid time is distributed between men and women and across different social groups will serve to narrow or widen inequalities (Coote et al., 2010; Goodwin, 2010).

For this and other reasons, transactions in the core economy can privilege some people over others (for example, where better-off parents share a car pool to ferry children to career-enhancing after-school activities). Individuals and groups may be excluded or disempowered because of how much discretionary time they have, where they come from, where they live, or their state of health. Some neighbourhoods seem to be awash with activities that enrich and strengthen social connections, while some appear beset by divisions or distrust, or have less opportunity for social exchange because, for example, there are no meeting places, or populations are transient, or fear of violence keeps people indoors. In many places, these positive and negative tendencies exist side by side. Some ethnic and cultural groups have stronger traditions than others of self-help and mutual aid, although these may go hand-in hand with values and customs that perpetuate inequalities (such as class-based snobbery, racial prejudice, or subordination of women).

It therefore matters a great deal how the core economy develops. This will affect not only the prospects for a new settlement, but also the quality of people's daily lives and relationships, the distribution of power and resources between them (especially between women and men), their physical and mental health and their future opportunities. Such changes can either exacerbate social divisions and inequalities, or help to promote sustainable social justice and well-being for all.

What are the benign options, then, for growing the core economy? For a start, it surely depends on devolving power and encouraging local action wherever possible. This is partly about formal devolution, with more power for local authorities and, within them, for neighbourhood-based decision-making bodies. It is also about opening up opportunities for people to take control over what happens in their own localities and providing access to resources that will make local action feasible and effective. This would need to go hand in hand with measures to encourage the fair distribution of opportunities and resources between localities. But even assuming a degree of equality between localities, the prospect of more devolution and local control begs further questions: who has power to participate and benefit? What makes some people powerful and others less so? And what can be done to help spread that power across the population?

It is beyond the scope of this paper to examine the full range of options for distributing power. I shall focus next on one essential determinant of power: our control over time. If we want to grow the core economy and promote co-production, we must pay attention to how we understand, value and distribute paid and unpaid time.

# Redistributing paid and unpaid time

In 1930, John Maynard Keynes imagined that by the beginning of the twenty-first century, the normal working week could be cut dramatically – to 15 hours. He anticipated that, because of increased productivity, we would no longer need to work long hours to earn enough to satisfy our material needs; our attention would turn instead to 'how to use freedom from pressing economic cares' (Keynes, 1963). Keynes was spectacularly wrong in his forecast. He did not anticipate the ways in which global capitalism would drive up accumulations of wealth, widen inequalities and turbo-charge consumption, enshrining a long-hours culture in most of the developed world. He was not wrong to anticipate the importance of using time differently.

There is nothing natural or inevitable about what are considered 'normal' patterns of time-use today. Time, like work, has become structured and commodified quite recently. Prevailing ideas about what is the appropriate length of the working day and week, what constitutes full-time and part-time employment, and where people should be at different times of day and night are a legacy of industrial capitalism, when the factory hooter sounded and workers clocked in and out. The logic of industrial time is out of step with today's working conditions, when instant communications and mobile technologies make it easy to insinuate all kinds of work into all corners of life, bringing new pressures as well as opportunities. The old industrial clock still ticks away in our heads, yet there are strong grounds for moving in the direction that Keynes envisaged: a gradual shift towards much shorter 'normal' working hours for workers of all kinds.

The case is set out in some detail in a report for the new economics foundation, *21 Hours: why a shorter working week can help us all to flourish in the 21st century* (Coote et al., 2010). In a nutshell, we argue that moving incrementally towards shorter and more flexible paid working hours will help to tackle the triple crises that currently beset the environment, the economy and society.

For the environment, a reduction in the standard working week will encourage those of us in paid employment to think again about how much money and stuff is enough, helping us to get off the consumer treadmill that so often shapes our lives and aspirations. Instead of living to work and working to earn and earning to consume and consuming in ways that are wrecking the planet, we'll have more time to live sustainably – to walk and cycle instead of travelling by car, to take the train instead of the plane, to mend things that break instead of buying new ones, to cook our own meals instead of buying processed ready-meals. We might think again about what we really value – for example, spending time with loved ones, learning more, reflecting, inventing, looking after each other, getting to know our neighbours and co-producing local activities. These things take up our time and are likely to improve the quality of our lives, but they involve little or no carbon-intensive consumption.

Shorter working hours will help to build an economy that can flourish without depending on unremitting growth. One effect of an economy that isn't growing is widespread unemployment. Cutting the hours of people in employment will help to create more jobs and to spread opportunities for paid work more evenly across the population. People who work shorter hours tend to be more productive hour for hour and less prone to stress, anxiety and other kinds of job-related illness. There would be less absenteeism and sick leave, which are costly for employers. And as working hours become more family-friendly there will be more women in employment and more men living rounded lives, offering skills and experience gained outside the workplace. These changes will help to build a more creative, stable workforce, which in turn is good for business.

Under favourable conditions (discussed below) a shorter working week will help to distribute paid and unpaid time more evenly between women and men. As I have noted above, women by all accounts spend more time than men doing unpaid work in the 'core economy'. This has happened in spite of a massive influx of women into paid employment over the last three decades. Profoundly entrenched assumptions about what are 'natural' patterns of employment and time-use for women and men affect the types of work they do, the hours they spend in paid employment and the value attached to their respective occupations. As a consequence, women continue to be channelled towards a narrow range of paid occupations that are seen as 'women's jobs', to command lower pay in the labour market and – often because of this – to 'choose' to take time out when they have children, leaving their higher-earning partner in full-time employment while they do the childcare and housework. There is a circular effect, reinforcing norms and expectations, perpetuating inequalities in income, time use and opportunities, and shoring up the general assumption (if not the reality) that men are the main breadwinners for their families. In a world where market-based values predominate, this combination leaves women with less money and power than men, and little scope for doing things differently (Bryson, 2007; Perrons, 2009).

Changing expectations about what is 'normal' could help, over time, to change attitudes and patterns of time use, and gradually to break down gendered divisions of labour. It could help fathers to be more engaged with their children, which would benefit children and mothers as well as the fathers themselves (Fatherhood Institute Research Summary, 2011; Hauari and Hollingworth, 2009).

Family relationships and unpaid time are vital components of the core economy. If we want to promote co-production as a key feature of a new well-being settlement, it will be essential to distribute paid and unpaid time more fairly across the population and particularly between women and men. Otherwise, there is a real danger that efforts to grow the 'core economy' and promote co-production will make women's lives harder and widen gender inequalities.

*Problems with redistributing time*

However positive and varied the benefits of moving to a shorter working week, there are bound to be serious difficulties in making the transition. The most obvious challenge is that a shorter working week would reduce the amount of money people can earn. Those on low rates of pay would be hardest hit. It could be seen as adding to the burden of people who are already poor and powerless. Many now have to work very long hours just to make ends meet.

The problem of low pay needs to be addressed urgently, regardless of hours of work. There should be a higher minimum hourly wage, lower taxes and better benefits for the low paid, as well as secure universal health and education services. Change would need to be incremental, with gradual reductions in working hours over a decade or more, giving people a chance to adapt their expectations and lifestyles. Policy-makers would have time to implement anti-poverty measures, and to introduce a range of flexible options to suit different people's needs (such as job-sharing, school term shifts, extended carer's leave and sabbaticals). It would also provide opportunities to trade productivity gains, year on year, for more time rather than just for more money.

I would not argue that these are *solutions* to the problems associated with moving to shorter working hours; only that change is *possible.*

# Moving from cure to prevention

I want to finish by making the case for moving 'upstream' to focus resources and action on preventing harm before it happens, rather than waiting to deal with the consequences once harm has occurred. This is another essential component of a new settlement for the 21st century. It applies not only to preventing social harm, but also to preventing harm to the environment and to the economy. I have set out the case for prevention on all three fronts, showing how these are inter-related, in *The Wisdom of Prevention* (Coote, 2012). I will touch briefly here on the social dimension and why prevention matters for social justice.

The case for a preventative approach is built on four ambitions: to improve people's quality of life (few of us want to be needy and vulnerable), to make more effective use of scarce public funds, to pre-empt the need for curative state intervention over time, and to help safeguard the life chances of future generations. It calls for long-term planning, a commitment to intergenerational equity and a revival of the principles of social solidarity; it requires a shared purpose, wise investment of shared resources and early action to tackle the underlying causes of harm. As Michael Marmot shows in his classic work on health inequalities, the primary causes of most social problems can be traced to the same bundle of issues: material poverty combined with a poverty of opportunity and aspiration, locked in by class, culture and location (Marmot, 2010).

The ideals of Beveridge were certainly preventative in spirit. When he planned a free national health service, he saw it as a fundamental upstream investment that would help prevent illness and therefore reduce expenditure on healthcare in future. He didn't foresee the complex ways in which, over time, new technologies, profit-driven pharmaceutical companies, powerful professional interests and an ageing population would fuel expectations and demands, driving up costs inexorably. Nor did he forsee that a national health service could deteriorate into an illness service, where patients do little more than proffer their bodies as a kind of tiltyard for clinicians to joust with malfunction and disease.

A similar process has taken place across the welfare state. Beveridge's vision of universal measures to protect us all against life's risks and misfortunes was a powerful expression of social solidarity. It has been corrupted over the intervening decades, so that we are left with the deficit model I described earlier: services provided by paid professionals to individuals who have problems and needs. Increasingly, these have been reserved for people who are vulnerable, needy or at risk. As resources have become scarcer, only those with more extreme vulnerabilities, needs and risks have been able to qualify as appropriate recipients. That means services don't kick in until the harm has already been done and probably left to fester for some time. By this time, the individuals involved have become *the problem:* it is they who are the (often stigmatised) focus of intervention, rather than the factors that shaped their problems in the first place. On the whole, these services don't work very well. They do next to nothing to prevent needs and problems recurring, to reduce demand for services, or to curb the upward spiral of costs.

My point is not that downstream curative measures are unnecessary. All too often they are essential. But without a stronger focus on prevention, efforts to cope with harm will have only limited scope or short-term success, because they will be confounded by factors further upstream that remain undisturbed. In a nutshell, it is essential to the pursuit of social justice that we give higher priority to preventing harm - for two inter-related reasons. First, it helps to cast a much-needed spotlight on the underlying causes of poverty and other social problems, and their unequal distribution. Secondly, it acknowledges that individuals seldom bear sole responsibility for disadvantages they face, and that if we want to promote a fairer and more equal society, we need to change underlying systems and structures, not just individual behaviour.

*Problems with prevention*
On the surface, being in favour of preventing harm is like being against sin. It has also been described as 'a category-shifting, mind-changing idea' (Robinson 2011). As with growing the 'core economy' and redistributing time, there are some formidable barriers that will need to be addressed.

For one thing, the logic of prevention seems to contradict the 'rescue principle' that defines philanthropy, charity and most health care. People who want to do good in the world are committed to helping those who are already needy. They may see upstream measures as a diversion. To tackle this problem we must change professional cultures, build up skills, knowledge and experience, and challenge the ethics of failing to prevent harm.

In addition, rescue and cure tend to have immediate, tangible and measurable results, while preventative measures are long-term, more complex and harder to measure. This creates a political bias against shifting the balance of investment upstream. Meanwhile, the neo-liberal consensus favours maximum freedom for markets and minimum state intervention. At the very moment when we most need to move upstream, for social, environmental and economic reasons, the ideas that shape our economy and politics are still pulling strongly in the opposite direction. This is unsustainable.

## In conclusion: conditions for radical change

The transition to a new settlement will need to be steady and incremental, winning public confidence through dialogue and partnership at every stage. Progress is unlikely to be swift or smooth. But let's not forget what a sorry state we are in, how very slim the chances are of returning to 'business as usual', and how thoroughly unjust and unsustainable 'business as usual' has been. In spite of the problems set out above, this may be the best chance in 30 years to grow the core economy, promote co-production, move towards much shorter working hours and put the wisdom of prevention at the heart of a new political economy.

We tend to think that social norms are deeply entrenched and very hard to shift, but there are many instances of attitudes changing dramatically over a relatively short period of time. Examples include ending the slave trade and slavery, giving votes to women, passing laws enforcing equal pay and opportunity, wearing crash helmets and seatbelts, corresponding by email, using mobile phones, not smoking in bars and restaurants, and seeing global warming as a serious man-made threat to the planet. In each case, the weight of public opinion shifted quite suddenly from one end of the spectrum (outrage, antipathy or indifference) to the other (acceptance, approval, staunch support), and reversing the change soon became almost inconceivable. This usually occurred when certain things coincided: new evidence, strong campaigning, and changing circumstances. Sometimes a sense of crisis can help to tip the weight of opinion – for example, to accept rationing in wartime or to see it as a fine thing to bring banks into public ownership when they are on the verge of collapse.

There is mounting evidence that unfettered markets are failing and that the post-war settlement is no longer able to fulfil its initial promise. We are building a substantial knowledge base about the potential effects of the changes I have outlined. Voices that dissent from the neoliberal consensus are growing stronger and more plentiful. We face a toxic combination of social, environmental and economic crises that are unique in history. It would seem, therefore, that conditions are ripe for change.

# References

Allen G and Duncan Smith I (2009) *Early Intervention: Good parents, Great Kids, Better Citizens*, Centre for Social Justice.

Bevan S and Jones A (2003) *Where's Daddy: The UK fathering deficit*. London: Work Foundation.

Bok S (2010) *Exploring happiness from Aristotle to brain science*. Yale: Yale University Press.

Boyle D and Harris M (2009) *The challenge of co-production*. London: NESTA/nef.

Boyle D, Slay J and Stephens L (2009) *Public services inside out*. London: NESTA/nef.

Boyle D, Coote A, Sherwood C et al. (2010) *Right here right now*. London: NESTA/nef.

Bryson V (2007) *Gender and the politics of time: Feminist theory and contemporary debates*. Bristol: Policy Press.

Burchardt T (2008) *Time and income poverty*, CASE Report 57. London: London School of Economics.

Cahn E (2001) *No more throwaway people: The co-production imperative*. Washington DC: Essential Books.

Coote A (2010) *Cutting It: The 'Big Society' and the New Austerity*. London: nef.

Coote A (2012) *The Wisdom of Prevention*. London: nef.

Coote A and Franklin J (2009) *Green Well Fair*. London: nef.

Coote A, Franklin J and Simms A (2010) *21 Hours*. London: nef.

Daycare Trust (2010) Summary of the Childcare costs survey. Available at: www.daycaretrust.org.uk/pages/summary-of-the-childcare-costs-survey-2010.html (accessed 15 December 2011).

Fatherhood Institute Research Summary (2011) Fathers, Mothers, Work and Family. Available at www.fatherhoodinstitute.org/index.php?id=10&cID=627 (accessed 15 December 2011).

Goodwin N (2010) If US consumption declines will the global economy collapse? In: Ekström, K. and Glans, K. (eds.) *Changing Consumer Roles*. New York: Routledge.

Goodwin N, Nelson J, Ackerman F et al. (2003) *Microeconomics in context.* New York: Houghton Mifflin.

Hauari H and Hollingworth K (2009) *Understanding fatherhood: masculinity, diversity and change.* York: Joseph Rowntree Foundation.

Hirsch D, Davis A and Smith N (2009) *A minimum income standard for Britain in 2009.* York: Joseph Rowntree Foundation.

Hochschild AR (2005) 'On the edge of the time bind: Time and market culture' *Social Research* 72(2): 339–354.

Jackson T (2009) *Prosperity without Growth.* London: Earthscan.

Jenks C (2005) *Childhood (Key Ideas),* 2nd edn. New York: Routledge.

Johnson P and Sibieta L (2011) 'Top income growth drives rise in income inequality under Labour' in IFS *Observations,* http://www.ifs.org.uk/publications/558

Keynes, JM (1963) *Essays in persuasion.* New York: W.W.Norton & Co, pp. 358–373.

Marmot M (2010) *Fair Society, Healthy Lives,* http://www.marmotreview.org/AssetLibrary/Exec%20sum%204.8MB.pdf

Michaelson J, Abdallah S, Steuer N et al. (2009) *National Accounts of Well-being.* London: **nef**.

Office of National Statistics (2011a) Annual Survey of Hours and Earnings (ASHE). Available at: www.ons.gov.uk/ons/rel/ashe/annual-survey-of-hours-and-earnings/ashe-results-2011/ashe-statistical-bulletin-2011.html (accessed 15 December 2011).

Office of National Statistics (2011b) Family Spending: a report on the 2010 Living Costs and Food survey. Available at: http://www.ons.gov.uk/ons/rel/family-spending/family-spending/family-spending-2011-edition/index.html (accessed 15 December 2011).

Parks RB, Baker PC, Kiser L et al. (1981) Consumers as coproducers of public services: Some economic and institutional considerations. *Policy Studies Journal* 9(7): pp. 1001–1011.

Perrons D (2009) *Women and gender equity in employment.* Working Paper, Institute for Employment Studies, UK, February.

Robinson D (2011) *Reimagining Prevention,* Community Links, October 3rd, http://www.community-links.org/linksuk/?cat=854

Slay J and Robinson B (2011) *In This Together: Building knowledge about co-production.* London: **nef**.

Spratt S, Simms A, Neitzert E et al. (2010) *The Great Transition: A tale of how it turned out right.* London: **nef**.

Timmins N (2001) *The five giants: A biography of the welfare state.* London: Harper-Collins.

Wann M (1995) *Building Social Capital.* London: ippr.

Workplace Options (2009) Work-Life Benefits 'Key to Employee Satisfaction'. Available at www.workplaceoptions.co.uk/news/press-releases/2009-21-Dec-work-life-balance-key-to-employee-satisfaction.asp (accessed 15 December 2011).

# Part Three

## Ireland and the future of the European Social Model

Does the European Social Model Have a Future?

# 5.

## The European Social Model and Ireland – Re-imagining for the twenty first century [39]

## Seán Healy, Brigid Reynolds, Michelle Murphy

*The European Commission's 1994 White Paper on social policy described the 'European social model' in terms of values that include democracy and individual rights, free collective bargaining, the market economy, equal opportunities for all, and social protection and solidarity. The model is based on the conviction that economic progress and social progress are inseparable: 'Competitiveness and solidarity have both been taken into account in building a successful Europe for the future.' …. the European social model features in the Treaty of the functioning of the European Union where it states that the Union, in all its activities 'shall aim to eliminate inequalities, and to promote equality, between men and women.' Further, it states that the Union, in defining and implementing its policies and activities, 'shall take into account requirements linked to the promotion of a high level of employment, the guarantee of adequate social protection, the fight against social exclusion, and a high level of education, training and protection of human health' (Article 9), and that the Union 'shall aim to combat discrimination based on sex, racial or ethnic origin, religion or belief, disability, age or sexual orientation' (Article 10).*

*The Treaty fully recognises the role of the social dialogue …. The European social model is considered to be unique in its dual focus on economic and social principles.*

European Foundation for the Improvement of Living and Working Conditions

---

[39] This chapter draws on a number of previous publications by the authors most notably Healy and Reynolds (2009 and 2010).

---

*February 24, 2012: As the European Central Bank (ECB) continued to pour billions of euro into rescuing banks who had gambled recklessly and lost their bets, the President of the ECB, Italian Mario Draghi, declared that "the European social model has already gone". In the course of a lengthy interview with the Wall Street Journal Draghi, a former Goldman Sachs banker who now commands the fate of Europe's single currency, stated there would be "no escape" from tough austerity measures in all of the over-indebted countries; and this will necessarily involve giving up the European social model based on job security and generous safety nets.* Presseurope.eu

# A question of purpose

The European social model in its various manifestations has always been concerned with securing the well-being of citizens. In recent years the issue of well-being has been the subject of much discussion and debate. Many reports have been produced by significant bodies in the policy-making process internationally and in Ireland. These include reports by the Organisation for Economic Cooperation and Development (OECD 2007, 2011), the New Economics Foundation (NEF, 2004, 2011, 2012), the Commission on the Measurement of Economic Performance and Social Progress (CMEPSP, 2008) and in Ireland, the National Economic and Social Council (NESC, 2009). These reports have all identified the importance of well-being for all societies and recognised that the purpose of public policy is ultimately to ensure the well-being of all members. Particular policies in specific economic, social, cultural, political or environmental areas are all measured by their ultimate capacity to contribute to the well-being of the members of society and to protecting the environment in which they live and on which they depend.

These reports and studies have identified a range of issues closely related to well-being. They include the issue of progress and how it should it be measured; helps and obstacles to well-being; the inter-relationship between human and ecological systems; the relative importance of economic growth and how it should be measured; the inter-relatedness or otherwise of economic growth, progress, the environment and well-being.

Flowing from these discussions there has been an emerging series of questions concerning the extent of the obligation on societies to promote the well-being of their members. How can the answers to such a question be decided? What are the implications of this obligation? What are the criteria by which this obligation is determined? Who should be involved in this discussion and who should make the final decisions? How can these be monitored on an on-going basis? How can directions be adjusted in light of emerging evidence?

A recent report by The National Economic and Social Council (NESC) defined well-being as follows: "A person's well-being relates to their physical, social and mental state. It requires that basic needs are met, that people have a sense of purpose, that they feel able to achieve important goals, to participate in society and to live the lives they value and have reason to value." (NESC 2009, p.xiii)[40] This is the well-being that *Social Justice Ireland* and the present authors would like for all members of all societies.

As far back as Plato it was recognised that the person grows and develops in the context of society. "Society originates because the individual is not self-sufficient, but has many needs which he can't supply himself"[41] (cited in George, V. 2010, p6). Down through the ages various philosophies and social arrangements have been proposed to meet the felt need in societies to fulfil their perceived obligations to their members. These varied from Aristotle's position of favouring private ownership but common use of property to ensure the dire needs of people were met, to the emphasis of both Plato and Aristotle that education should be free and compulsory, to Cicero's discussion of

---

[40] A summary of this report is included as a chapter in a previous volume in this series: Healy and Reynolds, 2009. That chapter was written by Helen Johnston of NESC who was the principal author of the report.

[41] (Plato, in Lee 1987, p58, cited in George, V. 2010, p6)

equality, to the early Christian emphasis on sharing and forming community.[42]

In more recent times the dignity of the person has been enshrined in The Universal Declaration of Human Rights which states: "All human beings are born free and equal in dignity and rights. They are endowed with reason and conscience and should act towards one another in a spirit of brotherhood." This core value is also at the heart of the Catholic Social Thought tradition. *Social Justice Ireland* and the authors in particular, support the values of both these traditions. We advocate that the dignity of each and every person must be recognised, acknowledged and promoted effectively. This implies that society's structures, institutions and laws should exist for the authentic development of the person.

The right of the individual to freedom and personal development is limited by the rights of other people. This leads to the second core value, namely, the common good. As we noted earlier the concept of the 'common good' originated over two thousand years ago in the writings of Plato, Aristotle and Cicero. More recently, the philosopher John Rawls defined the common good as "certain general conditions that are...equally to everyone's advantage" (Rawls, 1971 p.246). *Social Justice Ireland* understands the term 'common good' as "the sum of those conditions of social life by which individuals, families and groups can achieve their own fulfilment in a relatively thorough and ready way" (Gaudium et Spes no.74). This understanding recognises the fact that the person develops their potential in the context of society where the needs and rights of all members and groups are respected. The common good, then, consists primarily of having the social systems, institutions and environments on which we all depend, work in a manner that benefits all people simultaneously and in solidarity. The NESC study referred to already states that "at a societal level, a belief in a 'common good' has been shown to contribute to the overall well-being of society.

---

[42]  For an interesting review of the historical development of welfare see George, V. (2010), *Major Thinkers in Welfare: Contemporary Issues in Historical Perspective*, Bristol, The Policy Press.

This requires a level of recognition of rights and responsibilities, empathy with others and values of citizenship" (NESC 2009: 32).

This raises the issue of resources. The goods of the planet are for the use of all people – not just those in better-off countries; they are also for the use of generations still to come. The present generation must recognise it has a responsibility to ensure that it does not damage but rather enhances the goods of the planet that it hands on – be they economic, cultural, social or environmental. The structural arrangements regarding the ownership, use, accumulation and distribution of goods are disputed areas. However it must be recognised that these arrangements have a major impact on how society is shaped and how it supports the well-being of each of its members in solidarity with others.

In recent years many people have argued that the market will resolve these issues. They believe that following the economic recession the market is the only mechanism that can restore a sense of social obligation and develop a viable response to the questions raised above. Consequently, they argue that the primary focus of government policy should be to support and encourage business efficiency through the social, economic, cultural and political structures of society. This is an ideology that gives primacy to the economy. It believes that people should serve the economy, not vice versa.

On the other hand many others have argued that an untrammelled market undermines any reasonable attempt to shape society in the interest of securing every person's well-being. They believe that human dignity and human development are critically important as it is the right of every individual to realise his or her potential and aspirations. They look at history and say that the market has created inequalities rather than enhanced solidarity; that it has given huge priority to creating what is superfluous rather than redistributing necessities.

The authors believe that the economy should serve people and not the other way around. However, it is very important to note that we do not reject the market or the social role of private enterprises or profit or finance etc. and their capacities to contribute positively to the well-being of society and its members. Rather, we believe that the market should be at the service of people and that all can contribute to deciding the aims and choosing the priorities that ensure that the market in its various manifestations is at the service of securing every person's well-being while respecting and protecting the environment on which current and future generations depend.

## The welfare state

Down through the ages societies have struggled with these issues and responded to the challenge of securing and supporting the well-being of their members in a variety of ways. One approach to securing everyone's well-being has been the development of the welfare state.

According to Anthony Giddens "Welfare states are those in which Government plays a key role in reducing inequalities through the provision or subsidising of certain goods and services. Welfare services vary across countries but often include education, healthcare, housing, income support, disability, unemployment and pensions." (Giddens, 2011:518) In recent years the future of the welfare state has been discussed and debated across much of the 'developed' world. *Social Justice Ireland*'s annual Social Policy Conference in 2010 addressed this topic and the papers of that conference should be read in tandem with this chapter and indeed with the other chapters in this book (Reynolds et al, 2010).

Most countries either are or aspire to be welfare states in today's world. The services provided or sought in each welfare state and the proportion of a nation's income spent on them vary widely. There has been much discussion on what the exact differences between countries are and on why they have emerged. Marxists see welfare as necessary for the survival of capitalism. Functional theorists see welfare systems as integrating the various parts of society and ensuring that all can deal with the difficulties and complexities of modern societies.

# History and Frameworks

T.H. Marshall (1973) understood the welfare state to have emerged from a broadening understanding of citizenship and the rights that went with being a citizen. In the eighteenth century *civil rights* had emerged. These included rights such as freedom of speech, freedom of thought and freedom of religion as well as the right to own property and to fair legal treatment. These were followed in the nineteenth century by the emergence of *political rights* for citizens. These included the right to vote, to hold public office and to participate in the political process. Marshall saw the twentieth century as having produced *social rights*. These included the right to economic and social security through education, housing healthcare, pensions and other services. These are often referred to as social, economic and cultural rights. This third stage in the development of rights led to the acceptance of the view that everyone was entitled to sufficient income to live a full, active life irrespective of their background. The acknowledgement of social, economic and cultural rights advanced the idea of equality for all and promoted the goal of tackling inequality in society.

Marshall's interpretation was based on his experience of the UK. The evolutionary path he set out was not replicated by experience in other countries. Turner (1990) showed that countries such as Sweden, France and Germany had travelled different pathways towards these rights. There is also disagreement on whether or not Marshall saw his analysis as a description of what happened in the evolution of rights in the UK or whether he believed it to be a causal analysis that was, in effect, an evolutionary process. Either way, his core point that rights and responsibilities are closely linked with the idea of citizenship has been very popular in recent years as the idea of 'active citizenship' has been promoted.

Marshall's understanding of an evolving and expanding set of rights linked to citizenship continues to exercise major influence. Some would go so far as to argue that the evolution of rights continues and they point to the emergence of rights and responsibilities towards the environment (called *environmental or ecological rights*) as a further development in this process.

G. Esping-Andersen (1990) took Marshall's work a major step further. He analysed how different countries had taken different pathways to securing these rights for their citizens. In the process he concluded that there were three major approaches that produced three different 'welfare regimes'. Esping-Andersen based his analysis on the concept of 'decommodification' – "which simply means the degree to which welfare services are free from the market" (Giddens 2011: 507). Where decommodification is high then welfare is secured by the State and is not linked to one's income or economic resources. In a situation where decommodification is low then welfare services are available through the market like other goods and services.

Comparing government policies in three areas, pensions, income support and unemployment, Esping Andersen concluded there were three types of welfare state: *social democratic, conservative-corporatist and liberal.* The first two are highly decommodified but they differ from each other in that states following the democratic model provide many universal benefits (i.e. they are available to all citizens) while those in the conservative-corporatist model do not.

Scandinavian countries such as Sweden and Norway are examples of the social democratic approach while Germany, France and Austria follow the conservative-corporatist approach. Access to welfare in the latter countries is strongly linked to ones position in society, particularly one's record of paid employment. The argument has been made that the conservative-corporatist approach is not very interested in eliminating inequalities in society, but rather is focused on securing social stability strong families and loyalty to the state.

The liberal approach is different. It is highly commodified i.e. welfare services are available through the market and all are expected to buy their own services in that market. For those unable to do so means-tested benefits are available but usually for a limited time only. These benefits become stigmatized and dependence on them is seen as a sign of personal failure. The USA is the major example of this approach in practice.

This typology has been developed further since Esping Andersen produced his original work. Several southern European countries did not develop their welfare states until the nineteen seventies and eighties. These countries spend less of their public expenditures on welfare services even though this expenditure did increase dramatically towards the end of the last century; they have a strong focus on pensions and a low level of social assistance. These countries place strong conditionality on access by their citizens to social provision. They have rigid employment protection legislation and frequently resort to early retirement policies as a means of improving employment conditions. They could be seen as a fourth 'type' beside the three 'types' identified by Esping-Andersen.

A further additional category to those identified by Esping-Andersen can be seen in many of the EU's newest members who have fewer social protections. Coming out of the former Soviet Union they have a very different tradition which is not reflected as typical of their development in any of the four typologies identified above.

Ireland has a mixture of the liberal and conservative-corporatist approaches but has been tending ever more strongly towards the liberal model.

# The European Social Model Today

For Marshall, social citizenship provided a mechanism to correct the injustices caused by the capitalist market. He understood clearly that civil and political rights, on their own, simply were not sufficient to protect people against social and economic exclusion. The welfare state, however, with its social, economic and cultural rights would provide such protection. This protection, in turn, would secure social cohesion and solidarity as well as a productive economy and market. In practice this was the path followed by European welfare states in the decades following World War II.

In the quarter century before the crash of 2007/8 many countries increased their social spending. Between 1980 and 2005, for example, the 'Anglo-Saxon' countries along with other low-spend countries increased their social spending by about one fifth (as a percentage of GDP). Scandinavian countries were starting from a much higher base but they increased their spending by a similar amount. Japan increased its social spending by 75 per cent (principally to meet the needs of its aging population). The Mediterranean countries, which lagged behind other EU countries, had the fastest growing welfare states. Greece, Spain, Portugal and Italy increased their welfare effort by two-thirds in this period. Other countries in Western Europe saw their spending grow at a more modest rate. On average gross public expenditure on welfare across OECD countries increased from 16 per cent of GDP in 1980 to 21 per cent in 2005 (Adema and Ladaique 2009).

Another development that needs to be noted in this context is that spending on social policy rose as a share of public spending across the Western world in the second half of the twentieth century. Spending on defence was reduced as a proportion of public spending and industrial subsidies were reduced as major basic industries were privatised.

Despite these developments there has been an on-going debate on the future of the welfare state and of the European Social Model for the best part of 30 years. Developments such as faltering economies, changing demographics, globalisation, migration and many more have fuelled these debates at different times. There is general agreement in the literature that the European Social Model has been changing in terms of both its purpose (ends) and its means. The positive and negative nature of these developments is disputed. Some have concluded that it has been very effective at resisting attempts to reduce its scope (Mishra, 1990; Pierson,

1994; Timonen, 2003). Others argue that it has seen substantial reduction in recent decades (Bryson, 1992; Leonard, 1997; Jamrozik, 2001).

One major change that is generally recognised is in the whole understanding of 'work' on which the European Social Model and the Welfare State has been extensively based. From a situation of jobs for life, paying a 'family wage' in a world of near-full employment, today the world of jobs is characterised by flexibility, risk and precariousness for a large and growing proportion of the labour force.

A second major change is in the movement from 'passive benefits' to 'social investment' in human capital. There is a strong emphasis on 'activation' programmes and people find they must participate in training or some form of 'make-work' schemes to access their benefits. In Scandinavian countries there has always been a strong emphasis on vocational training and activation but they have, and continue to, combine this with a strong commitment to the universal principle. Those following the 'liberal' approach have tended to reduce universalism more and more.

The emerging European Social Model sees a realignment between these three areas i.e. work, social investment and active participation. However, there is a flaw at the core of this process. It gives major priority to the individual and places great emphasis and faith in the individual's capacity to generate collective good. In fact, it places responsibility for securing social cohesion and solidarity on the individual rather than on society and the state. This is a fundamental change from Marshall's understanding of citizenship rights and their associated social justice norms. It should not be an either/or choice. Both the individual and the state have essential roles to play if the European Social Model is not to fade away or just apply to the privileged. Some commentators have argued that there was too great an emphasis on the State's responsibilities at the expense of the individual. A rebalancing should not lead to a major reduction in the State's responsibilities. As part of the current global adjustment the State's role is being cut back; social protection is being reduced; safety nets are being reduced or removed. Downplaying the role of the state will simply deliver more unequal participation and lead to further inequalities. This is a critical issue for the future of the European Social Model.

As the European Union expanded, its integration process created a constitutional disconnection between policies promoting market efficiencies and policies promoting social protection and equality. While the European social model was supposed to support both in an integrated manner, the Union in fact gave much greater priority to the market component. Rules and laws were put in place governing economic integration, liberalisation and competition law and these ensured that individual countries complied with these developments.

On the other hand far less priority was given to European social policies and countries were not bound by rules or laws that required improved performance on these issues. This weakness was recognised and the 'open method of coordination' was put in place in the area of social policy. This left decision-making on social policy issues to national parliaments but tried to improve these through promoting common objectives and common indicators as well as through comparative evaluations of national performance. Over a period of time it became clear that this approach was having little impact and the gap between how economic/market policy and social policy were viewed widened steadily. This is obvious when developments since 2000 are analysed.

In the year 2000 the European Union agreed a new strategy to become 'the most competitive and dynamic knowledge-based economy in the world capable of sustainable economic growth with more and better jobs and greater social cohesion'. The European social model was to be developed through investing in people and developing an active and dynamic welfare state. This was seen as crucial by the European Council so as to secure Europe's place in the knowledge economy and to ensure that the so-called new economy did not exacerbate social problems such as unemployment, social exclusion and poverty. This approach, known as the *Lisbon Strategy*, was substantially amended at its half-way point in 2005 and the issue of social cohesion was down-graded for the remaining five years of the strategy. By its conclusion date in 2010 the Lisbon

Strategy had clearly failed to deliver on either its economic or social goals. A new strategy was put in its place in 2010 called *Europe 2020*. While it contains targets on poverty, education, jobs and the environment, on the evidence of its initial years there is little confidence that it will get to grips with some of the major challenges that face the welfare state at this moment in history.

The financial and economic crisis of 2008 and following years has seen a huge increase in the pressures Governments across the Europe are facing on balancing their budgets. Many have urged substantial cuts in welfare provision and in social expenditure generally. The primary focus has been on moving the economy onto a sustainable path but this has been done for the most part without much reference to the European Social Model and its commitments on delivering services for people. Austerity is the order of the day and the pathways being followed by Governments are generally regressive in nature. While all citizens have been targeted to absorb part of the austerity there has been a general failure to recognise that those who are better off are in a far better situation to absorb these hits while those who are vulnerable have been forced to cut back far more than they can absorb.

Side by side with the economic crash of recent years there has been a growing awareness that there are environmental limits to what can be achieved. Many policies have been put into place that are not sustainable either environmentally or economically. There has been a rowing back on commitments which themselves were inadequate. The recently concluded Rio+20 conference produced an agreed statement that fell far short of what might be considered the minimum required to protect the environment and secure the future.

All of which suggests that 70 years after publication of the Beveridge Report a new 'settlement' is needed, a re-design or a re-imagining. What should that new 'settlement' include? The next section of this chapter sets out what we consider to be the key components of an updated European Social Model that would be appropriate for the changed world of the twenty first century.

# Key components of a
# 21<sup>st</sup> century European Social Model

## 1. An appropriate, secure income distribution system

The income distribution system that is seen as ideal at present involves all adults of working age having paid employment. This is supported by a welfare system that ensures people have a basic amount of money if they are unemployed, ill or otherwise unable to access income from having a job. This system has consistently failed to eliminate poverty. It has consistently failed to generate full employment on any kind of permanent basis. It needs to be radically overhauled to address the world of the 21<sup>st</sup> century.

The present authors have argued for a long time that the tax and social welfare systems should be integrated and reformed to make them more appropriate to the changing world of the twenty-first century. We suggest that the present system be replaced by a Basic Income system. A Basic Income is an income that is unconditionally granted to every person on an individual basis, without any means test or work requirement. In a Basic Income system every person receives a weekly tax-free payment from the Exchequer, and all other personal income is taxed, usually at a single rate.

For a person who is unemployed, the basic income payment would replace income from unemployment payments. For a person who is employed the basic income payment would replace tax credits in the income-tax system. Basic income is a form of minimum income guarantee that avoids many of the negative side effects inherent in the current social welfare system. A basic income differs from other forms of income support in that

- it is paid to individuals rather than households;
- it is paid irrespective of any income from other sources;
- it is paid without conditions; it does not require the performance of any work or the willingness to accept a job if offered one;
- it is always tax free.

A Basic Income system would replace welfare payments. It could guarantee an income above the poverty line for everyone. It would not be means tested. There would be no "signing on" and no restrictions or conditions. In practice a basic income recognises the right of every person to a share of the resources of society.

The Basic Income system ensures that looking for a paid job and earning an income, or increasing one's income while in employment, is always worth pursuing, because for every euro earned the person will retain a large part. It thus removes the many poverty traps and unemployment traps that may be in the present system. Furthermore, women and men get equal payments in a basic income system. Consequently the basic income system promotes gender equality.

Ensuring people's well-being requires a secure income system. Basic Income is a system that is altogether more guaranteed, rewarding, simple and transparent than the present tax and welfare systems. It is far more employment friendly than the present system.

A new system is required to secure an adequate income for all in the twenty-first century. Basic Income is such a system.

## 2. Recognition of all meaningful work, not just paid employment

Paid employment throughout their lifetime will not be available for all those in the labour force anytime in the foreseeable future. Yet everyone has a right to work. The importance of work for people's well-being is not disputed. However, the understanding of work has been narrowed in practice to paid employment. Other kinds of work which are not remunerated, such as care work, are not seen as 'real' work. This situation raises serious questions about the meaning and perception of work. The authors believe that meaningful work is essential for people's well-being. The authors believe that every person has the right to meaningful work. The challenge faced by many societies today is to ensure that right is honoured for all even if paid full-time jobs do not exist for all. We believe that it is possible to produce a situation where everyone has meaningful work even if full employment has not been achieved. It would involve the recognition of all forms of meaningful work, not just paid employment.

A major question raised by the current labour-market situation concerns *assumptions* underpinning culture and policy making in this area. One such assumption concerns paid employment which is assumed to be achievable in a relatively short time frame if only the correct policies were put in place. The reality raises serious questions concerning this assumption. There are hundreds of millions of people unemployed or underemployed across the world. Even in the most affluent countries there are many who are unemployed or under-employed. It is crucial that job-creation be promoted and that all that is possible be done to create well-paid jobs in which people do meaningful work. However, it is also crucial that societies face up to the fact that there will be many unemployed people for the foreseeable future. One possible pathway towards a solution might be to address a second assumption in the whole area of work.

This second assumption concerns the priority given to paid employment over other forms of work. Most people recognise that a person can work very hard even though they do not have a conventional job. Much of the work carried out in the community and in the voluntary sector fits under this heading. So too does much of the work done in the home. The authors' support for the introduction of a basic income system comes, in part, from a belief that all work should be recognised and supported.

There has been some progress on this issue particularly in the growing recognition of the value of voluntary work. The need to recognise voluntary work was acknowledged in the Government White Paper, *Supporting Voluntary Activity* (Department of Social, Community and Family Affairs, 2000). The national social partnership agreement *Towards 2016* also contains commitments in this area.

A report presented to the Joint Oireachtas Committee on Arts, Sport, Tourism, Community, Rural and Gaeltacht Affairs in 2005 established that the cost to the state of replacing the 475,000 volunteers working for charitable organisations would be a minimum of €205 million and could cost up to €485 million per year.

Government should more formally recognise and acknowledge all forms of work. We believe that everybody has a right to work, understood as contributing to his or her own development and/or that of the community and/or the wider society. However, we believe that policy making in this area should not be exclusively focused on job creation. Policy should recognise that access to meaningful work is an important factor in human well-being. A Basic Income system would create a platform for meaningful work. It would benefit paid employment as well as other forms of work.

## 3. A strong focus on strengthening participation by all

The need to strengthen participation by all has two aspects. One concerns participation in development at an economic and/or social level. This has been addressed to some extent under the preceding item i.e. the need to value all work. The second aspect concerns participation at a political level. Participation in both of these ways is important for people's well-being. Both should also be essential aspects of any future European Social Contract.

Democracy means 'rule by the people'. This implies that people participate in shaping the decisions that affect them most closely. This is a significant feature of individual and societal well-being according to Amartya Sen (Sen, 1999). This includes people having the freedom and the processes to express themselves politically and creatively. While we live in a democracy and freedom of expression is accepted in theory at least, there are problems with the current model. What we have, in practice, is a highly centralised government in which we are 'represented' by professional politicians. The more powerful a political party becomes, the more distant it seems to become from the electorate. Party policies on a range of major issues are often difficult to discern. Backbenchers have little control over, or influence on, government ministers, opposition spokespersons or shadow cabinets. Even within the cabinet some ministers seem to be able to ignore their cabinet colleagues. This makes participation in real terms difficult.

The democratic process has certainly benefited from the participation of various sectors in other arenas such as social partnership. It would also benefit from the development of a new social contract against exclusion and a new forum for dialogue on civil society issues.[43] However there is also a need to move towards deliberative democracy and to develop structures where power differentials are neutralised. This would produce a situation where far more emphasis was given to the analysis of situations, to the alternatives proposed and to the implementation pathways being identified. We now reflect on two relevant issues specifically – firstly on shared social responsibility and secondly on social dialogue.

### Shared social responsibility is a key component of the policy-making and policy-delivery process

If a pathway is to be found to securing everyone's well-being through the welfare state or through any other means, the issue of responsibility must be addressed. If a democratic society is to function effectively then the exercise of responsibility is both a right and an obligation. Given the current situation of crisis across the world in so many contexts e.g. economic, political, cultural, environmental and social, and given the collapse of confidence in key institutions ranging from the economy to church, from banking to the legal to politics, the issue of responsibility needs to be debated.

Nation states and the world itself are facing huge challenges to rebuild confidence and to find credible responses to the challenges already identified in this chapter. To achieve this it is essential that the understanding of responsibility for the well-being of all be re-defined and broadened. It should be understood as meaning a responsibility that

---

[43] For a further discussion of these issues see Healy and Reynolds (2003: 191-197).

is shared by all, that is exercised by all in the context of their capacity and capability. It should also mean that this responsibility is shared by individuals, by institutions and by society generally, including governments. Given the inter-dependence of so much of modern life and the process of globalisation it is crucial that people and nation states recognise the global nature of many of the problems they face and recognise that addressing these effectively requires that all accept they have a shared responsibility for developing and implementing a viable alternative to the present system.

Sharing responsibility must be at the core of any credible pathway forward. We have argued already in this chapter that the economy should be at the service of people, of the present and future generations, rather than people being at the service of the economy. A viable future also requires conservation of the planet as the common home of humanity and of life in general. None of this will happen unless there is a new approach that recognises and acts on the need for an approach based on shared responsibility.

There are many rights that have been secured in the European Convention on Human Rights and Fundamental Freedoms, the revised European Social Charter and the European Union's Charter of Fundamental Rights; likewise, with the UN Declaration on Human Rights and other similar instruments. But actually having those rights vindicated and delivered in practice requires that responsibilities to others alive today and in the future be recognised and addressed pro-actively.

In finding a way out of the current series of crises it is crucial that the unequal impact of these crises on different groups be recognised. Poor and/or vulnerable people suffered most as a result of these crises. These are the same people who bear least responsibility for the mechanisms which produced these crises. In many cases they are the people who have to pay a lot more tax to rescue these mechanisms (such as the banking system) and who see the services provided by the welfare state eroded as governments' finances are re-directed to the rescue of these same banks. In practice what this situation shows is that some people who have more power and information are able to minimise or eliminate their own responsibility for what happens while vulnerable people who have no say and did not cause the problems are left carrying much more of the responsibility.

If there is to be a viable, desirable future where everyone's well-being is secured and promoted then it is crucial that social responsibilities be shared more fairly between governments, citizens, business, civil society, faith communities and all others involved in any manner. All actors should be involved in developing a shared vision of the future based on some shared values and developing pathways towards that vision at a wide range of levels. For this to happen, a genuinely participatory process is required. As we have outlined already we favour a deliberative process in which power differentials are neutralised.

In arguing for shared social responsibility to be at the core of a new approach, we see social responsibility going far beyond the obligation to answer for ones actions; it also includes approaching issues with a perspective that includes promoting the well-being of others including future generations. We also realise that not everyone can be involved in shaping all decisions. However, we believe shared social responsibility involves a commitment to generating a consensus concerning both the vision and the pathways and then involving people in different situations in deciding how best to move forward within these parameters. In practice this requires major reorganising at the political, economic and social levels. In recent decades the demand for autonomy and for freedom of choice produced an approach that relied to a great extent on self-regulation of individuals and markets. That model has failed. We now require an approach that links autonomy, as the ability of each individual to manage his/her own existence in accordance with a freely chosen lifestyle, to social justice in which individual preferences are balanced against the group interest and each person's fundamental rights.

*Social dialogue is a key part of policy development*
*and includes all major sectors of society on an equal basis.*
One mechanism for sharing responsibility in decision-making and subsequent implementation concerns the process of social dialogue. Taoiseach, Enda Kenny has commented[44] that he saw "an important role for social dialogue in helping to broaden understanding about what needs to be done". This statement is welcome. So too is the Taoiseach's insistence that social dialogue "must facilitate, not strangle or frustrate, change and reform" is also welcome. However, it would be totally unacceptable for Government to introduce a process of social dialogue that would benefit the rich and exclude the rest of us. A recent proposal[45] for social dialogue made by a leading trade unionist would see social dialogue involving trade unions and employers **only**, and excluding the rest of society. This would be a recipe for ensuring that most of Ireland's resources would be captured by the public sector and the corporate sector or, to be more precise, if past performance were to be a guide, it would mean that the major beneficiaries would be the better paid in the public sector and large corporations. Such an approach would simply lead to deepening divisions and growing inequality in Ireland.

Government needs to engage all sectors of society, not just trade unions and employers, in addressing the huge challenges Ireland currently faces. If government wishes the rest of us to take responsibility for producing a more viable future then it must involve the rest of us. Responsibility for shaping the future should be shared among all stakeholders. There are many reasons for involving all sectors in this process e.g. to ensure priority is given to well-being and the common good; to address the challenges of markets and their failures; to link rights and responsibilities; to secure the environment for future generations.

---

[44]  Irish Times, May 19, 2012
[45]  ibid

---

When groups have been involved in shaping decisions they are far more likely to take responsibility for implementing these decisions, difficult as they may be. A process of Social Dialogue is a key mechanism in maximising the resources for moving forward.

## 4. Sustainability (economic, environmental and social) at the core of all policy-making

The search for a humane, sustainable model of development has gained momentum in recent times. After years of people believing that markets and market forces would produce a better life for everyone, major problems and unintended side effects have raised questions and doubts. There is a growing awareness that sustainability must be a constant factor in all development, whether social, economic or environmental.

This fact was reiterated by Kofi Annan, the then-Secretary-General of the United Nations, at the opening of the World Summit on Sustainable Development in Johannesburg, South Africa (September 2002). There he stated that the aim of the conference was to bring home the uncomfortable truth that the model of development that has prevailed for so long has been fruitful for the few, but flawed for the many. And he further added that the world today, facing the twin challenges of poverty and pollution, needs to usher in a season of transformation and stewardship – a season in which we make a long overdue investment in a secure future.

Sustainable development has been defined in many different ways. Perhaps the best- known definition is that contained in Our Common Future (World Commission on Environment and Development, 1987:43): *development that meets the needs of the present without compromising the ability of future generations to meet their own needs.*

It is crucial that the issues of environmental, economic and social sustainability be firmly at the core of the decision making process if the well-being of all, today and into the future, is to be realised. Principles to underpin sustainable development were suggested in a report for the European Commission prepared by James Robertson in May 1997. Entitled *The New Economics of Sustainable Development*, the report argues that these principles would include the following:

- systematic empowerment of people (as opposed to making and keeping them dependent) as the basis for people-centred development
- systematic conservation of resources and environment as the basis for environmentally sustainable development
- evolution from a "wealth of nations" model of economic life to a "one-world" economic system
- evolution from today's international economy to an ecologically sustainable, decentralising, multi-level one-world economic system
- restoration of political and ethical factors to a central place in economic life and thought
- respect for qualitative values, not just quantitative values
- respect for feminine values, not just masculine ones.

At first glance, these might not appear to be the concrete guidelines that policy-makers so often seek. Yet they are principles that are relevant to every area of economic life. They also apply to every level of life, ranging from personal and household to global issues. They impact on lifestyle choices and organisational goals. They are at least as relevant today as they were when first proposed in 1997. If these principles were applied to every area, level and feature of economic life they would provide a comprehensive checklist for a systematic policy review.

## 5. What matters must be measured

A central initiative in putting sustainability at the core of development would be the development of "satellite" or "shadow" national accounts. Our present national accounts miss fundamentals such as environmental sustainability. Their emphasis is on GNP/GDP as scorecards of wealth and progress. These measures, which came into widespread use during

World War II, more or less ignore the environment, and completely ignore unpaid work. Only money transactions are tracked. They fail to register the benefits of the welfare state. On the other hand they do count its failures. For example, when children are cared for in the home no monetary value is added to GNP/GDP. On the other hand if the child is cared for in a crèche the costs involved are added. Even more dramatic costs are added if the child has to be cared for by the state. Similarly, while environmental depletion is ignored, the environmental costs of dealing with the effects of economic growth, such as cleaning up pollution or coping with the felling of rain forests, are added to, rather than subtracted from, GNP/GDP. New scorecards are needed.

If well-being is the purpose of the welfare state then it is important that data is collected and analysed on the main indicators of well-being. The OECD has done a great deal of work on this issue in recent years and produces a regular publication on social indicators called *Society at a Glance*. The OECD global project on measuring progress and some of the challenges it faces were addressed at some length in a recent publication in this series (Morrone, 2009). The OECD states that "social indicators aim to provide information on well-being beyond that conveyed by conventional economic measures" (OECD, 2007, p.20). Such indicators matter in the assessment of well-being. Measuring what matters should be a key component of the future welfare state.

## 6. Complete health should be promoted

Health is a major element of well-being. People's health is influenced by social conditions such as poverty, social exclusion, discrimination, inappropriate accommodation, a polluted environment and lack of community networks (World Health Organisation, 2004, 2011; Farrell et al., 2008). These are important determinants of most diseases, deaths and health inequalities between and within countries.

*"Health inequities arise from the societal conditions in which people are born, grow, live, work and age, referred to as social*

*determinants of health. These include early years' experiences, education, economic status, employment and decent work, housing and environment, and effective systems of preventing and treating ill health.... We are convinced that action on these determinants, both for vulnerable groups and the entire population, is essential to create inclusive, equitable, economically productive and healthy societies. Positioning human health and well-being as one of the key features of what constitutes a successful, inclusive and fair society in the 21st century is consistent with our commitment to human rights at national and international levels."* (WHO 2011: no.6)

Promoting complete health would involve addressing issues such as life expectancy, healthy life years, access to healthcare services, chronic illness, mental illness and many related aspects of health. It would also involve addressing the fact that people with lower levels of education or low income, for example, face a higher risk to their well-being. Producing such an approach to health is challenging at the present time. A major re-structuring and huge increases in public expenditure in Ireland are not seen to have delivered a better system or improved people's overall health or well-being.

The health system should take a 'whole of health' approach and consider its purpose to be the promotion of complete health, defined by the World Health Organisation as "a state of complete physical, mental and social well-being and not merely the absence of disease or infirmity." [46] A substantial proportion of the expenditure on health goes on medical provision. There is a need to move from a medical model to become more prevention oriented. There is still a long way to go. Far higher priority should be given to prevention, primary, community and continuing care.

---

[46] Preamble to the Constitution of the World Health Organisation as adopted by the International health Conference, New York, 19-22 June, 1946; signed on 22 July 1946 by the representatives of 61 states and entered into force on 7 April, 1948. This definition has not been amended since 1948.

## 7. The focus of education should be broadened to ensure it produces fully rounded human beings

Education is another essential part of people's well-being. It contributes to human flourishing by enabling people to acquire knowledge and develop their capabilities. It can promote well-being of the person by helping their own development and it can promote the well-being of society by engaging the person in development at that level. It is also closely linked to people's job opportunities. Education can be an agent for social transformation. It can be a powerful force in counteracting inequality and poverty. However, it needs to be acknowledged that, in many ways, the present education system has quite the opposite effect. Recent studies in Ireland confirm the persistence of social class inequalities which are seemingly ingrained in the system. Even in the context of increased participation and economic boom, the education system continues to mediate the vicious cycle of disadvantage and social exclusion between generations.

Early school leaving is a particularly serious manifestation of wider inequality in education, which is embedded in and caused by structures in the system itself. We believe that the core objective of education policy should be: to provide relevant education for all people throughout their lives, so that they can participate fully and meaningfully in developing themselves, their community and the wider society. Education should help to create capable and emotionally well-rounded people who are happy and motivated.

As in health, there should be a holistic approach to education. The curriculum should include the opportunity to cultivate the variety of 'intelligences' people have including musical, spatial, physical, interpersonal and intrapersonal.[47] The key should be the development of an education system focused on producing fully rounded human beings who can live in solidarity with other human beings and the environment in which they live.

---

[47] For further development of this issue see H. Gardner (1993).

## 8. Adequate and appropriate accommodation should be available for all

The availability of appropriate accommodation is essential in any model of a welfare state. A secure and pleasant place in which to live is a basic requirement for human flourishing. The official objective of Irish housing policy is "to enable every household to have available an affordable dwelling of good quality, suited to its needs, in a good environment, and as far as possible, at the tenure of its choice" (Department of Environment at www.environment.ie). Despite huge growth in the numbers of housing units built annually in Ireland in the period 1988-2006 (up from 14,204 dwellings to 93,419), Ireland failed to address its social housing needs problem. The number of households on local authority waiting lists more than doubled from 27,427 in 1996 to 56,249 in 2008. This failure was exacerbated by a housing price bubble which saw house prices rise dramatically. By 2012 the waiting list had risen above 100,000 households.

During the boom years Ireland experienced an astonishing growth in property construction and house prices. Construction became a major element in and driver of the Irish economy. However, housing construction increased at a rate which was not supported by demand. It was promoted as an end in itself. The result was a housing bubble which has contributed to the current economic crisis. Poor financial and planning regulations along with tax incentives served to support this negative phenomenon (Kitchin et.al 2010).

Central to the welfare state in the coming years should be an approach that sees housing as a home rather than a market commodity (Drudy, 2005, 2006). Drudy points out that there is a fundamental philosophical question that should be addressed concerning the purpose of a housing system. Should it be a system to provide investment or capital gains for those with the necessary resources or should its critical aim be to provide a home as a right for all citizens? In his view Ireland should move away from seeing housing as a commodity to be traded on the market like any other tradable commodity; and to accept the latter opinion that views housing as a social requirement like health services or education. This is a view with which the authors agree.


## 9. All cultures should be respected

Ensuring the welfare state is available to and benefits everyone is especially challenging in difficult economic times. This challenge can be even greater in a society with different cultures, different expectations and different understandings of well-being. Before the world developed affordable communication and travel systems people were divided because of their different cultures, values and beliefs. Centuries have passed and societies still have problems with the acceptance of others. In the recent past Ireland experienced substantial immigration as tens of thousands of people from abroad were needed to meet the employment needs of, and sought to benefit from, the 'Celtic Tiger'. A well-functioning welfare state focusing on the well-being of all would structure itself so that all can contribute to the underpinning values and meaning of society and have their own culture respected and valued in the process.


## 10. Social capital, civil society, social well-being and active citizenship should be recognised and strengthened in the policy development process.

Many of the aspects already outlined have implications for civil society, social well-being and active citizenship. Research produced in recent years shows the profound importance of communities and relationships in determining people's quality of life. Robert Putnam describes social capital as "features of social organisation, such as networks, norms and social trust that facilitate co-ordination and co-operation for mutual benefit". He argues that the major components of social capital are trust, norms, reciprocity and networks and connections. Social capital has been shown to have positive economic effects while also impacting on people's health and general well-being. It has also been shown that community engagement not only improves the well-being of those who are engaging in such activity but also improves the well-being of others.

In his perceptive analysis Tom Healy reminds us that David Myers defines well-being, at its simplest, as: 'the pervasive sense that life has been and is good. It is an on-going perception that this time in one's life, or even life as a whole, is fulfilling, meaningful, and pleasant.' However, Tom Healy goes on to point out that well-being goes well beyond mental states of pleasure, happiness or satisfaction for individuals, important as these are. Social well-being concerns the match between our goals and the kind of life we experience. In other words it concerns what we value and seek and how we evaluate our lives in this light. [48] Drawing on reflections from Aristotle to latter-day philosophers like Amartya Sen we can say that well-being involves coherence between the moral ends and chosen values of an individual or society, and the objective circumstances of life as perceived by them. The welfare state has a huge role to play in delivering such an outcome.

## Challenges to a 21st century European Social Model

There are a wide range of issues that need to be addressed if pathways are to be found towards an appropriate social model in the twenty first century. We wish to raise a critically important one here i.e. the issue of financing the European Social Model.

## The issue of financing in an age of fiscal austerity

We have discussed already the pressures that face any manifestation of the European Social Model in the years ahead. This situation is made even more challenging in the Eurozone as the Fiscal Compact becomes the law in each country. Many have argued that the Compact in practice will have a very negative impact on the welfare state generally, on the provision of social services and on the overall level of social expenditure.

---

[48]   For further elaboration on this see Tom Healy (2005)

The issue of financing is of critical importance. Idealism, aspiration and expectation must be matched by resources. If the social model cannot be funded in the future then it will not survive. In fact the political acceptability of any developments in the welfare state is closely linked to economic sustainability. While the world continues to be organised economically as a capitalist market economy there will be pressure to ensure that the cost of the welfare state does not fall too heavily on market enterprises so as not to impede free competition in production and trade. Despite benefiting generously from the advantages of the welfare state, the middle classes are often reluctant to support a generous level of redistribution. The cost of financing the various components of the welfare state has, for the most part, been rising. Simultaneously, the fact that people live longer has also been increasing the costs. There may well be further pressure on funding as improving living standards may lead some to feel they don't need the welfare state. At the same time there may be a growing tendency to reduce the redistribution element by providing support only for the 'deserving' poor.

These developments suggest the welfare state needs to provide a comprehensive rationale to explain and justify demands.

1. Firstly, there will be a growing demand for transparency. People will want to know precisely who is paying what for the welfare state and who is gaining what from it. This should be possible without too much difficulty given the world's improved technological capacity. However, the results will have to be reliable and verifiable. There have been some recent examples where the level of accuracy and of transparency left a great deal to be desired.
2. Secondly, there may be a demand to ensure social justice. This is not just an issue about adequacy, which of course is a critically important issue. There is also a need to ensure that the welfare state promotes the human dignity of participants and the common good as core values.
3. A third issue that has already arisen is the issue of people living longer. This would not be a problem for the welfare state as long as people extended their 'working' lives beyond the traditional retirement age.

In the 1980s a century-long process of reduction in the working age in the US was reversed. The UK saw a similar reverse emerge about 1995. More recently other OECD countries, including Ireland, have been following this trend. Another approach is the one adopted by Sweden and Germany where they reformed their pension systems and built in automatic reviews of the level of pension payments to ensure they remain in line with the increasing life expectancy. An interesting comparative statistic was produced by the UK's Pension Commission which showed that in 1950 the average male spent 17 per cent of his adult life in retirement. By 2000, it had risen to 31 per cent. The Commission argued that this could not continue to rise. They proposed that retirement be accepted as the norm for about 30 per cent of adult life and that the age when one becomes eligible for a state pension should be raised as required to meet this target.

4. A fourth aspect of the financing issue concerns its sustainability. For example, the EU countries will have to increase the percentage they spend on social welfare payments by about 4 per cent of GDP to meet the costs of current welfare payments and promises made for the future. When one extends the number of countries involved to include all OECD countries then the requirement rises to between 5 and 6 per cent. These increases are definitely feasible. Ireland is in a slightly different situation as its population is much younger and the ageing of the population experienced by most EU countries is still a few decades away. Given that Ireland's pension provision is far less generous than most EU-15 countries it should be possible to meet the rising costs with something to spare and remain a low-tax country.

5. A fifth aspect of financing in the future concerns alternatives to raising taxes. Different approaches are emerging where people are encouraged or forced to support their own social provision. In Sweden, for example, 2.5% of workers earnings must be invested in privately-funded pensions. Private health insurance is now compulsory in the Netherlands. Compulsory health insurance is also imposed in some states in the USA and the US government is moving towards near-universal healthcare coverage. Various forms of graduate taxes have been introduced to fund third level education.

6. A sixth area of activity in addressing the issue of financing has been and will continue to be the move to reduce or eliminate disincentives to taking up paid employment. Maximising labour-force participation is seen as the key to providing the funding required for the welfare state. So we may well see increased subsidisation for low-paid jobs and increased funding for training programmes for those who are unemployed. Some countries may move towards a workfare approach to labour market activation even though the evidence suggests that this is a high-cost route to take. Another approach might be the development of voluntary programmes where those in receipt of unemployment payments could work in the public or the community and voluntary (non-profit) sector doing real part-time jobs for the going hourly 'rate for the job'. They could work the required number of hours to receive their unemployment payment (up to a maximum of half the normal length of the working week) and then be free to take up any further employment that was available and pay tax in the normal way while maintaining their entitlements to supports such as a medical card.

Failure to address the financing issue could lead to a situation where a large proportion of a society's population was unable to provide privately for its welfare while no alternative was available to them. Historically, such a problem has led to the elimination of the existing social order and its replacement with some form of totalitarian, collectivist regime which in turn failed. The twentieth century has made great progress in recognising and supporting human rights. But rights can become an illusion unless the financing to deliver these rights is secured and sustained.

# What should Ireland do now?

## 1. On Income:

- Move towards a Basic Income system. Initial steps in this direction could see a Basic Income being available for children and for older people. This would mean that Government would maintain the current untaxed Child Benefit system and introduce a Universal State Pension, set perhaps at the current level of the Contributory State Pension.

- Reverse the current process whereby the resource of poor and middle-income people are being transferred to the rich. This process is clear in the Budget choices made by Government as it seeks to implement the Bailout Agreement.

## 2. On work:

- Formally recognise and acknowledge all forms of meaningful work, not just paid employment, as being worthwhile.

- Develop a major investment programme to maximise the number of worthwhile jobs available in Ireland.

- Introduce a part-time job opportunities programme that would enable those who are long-term unemployed voluntarily to take up part-time jobs in the community and voluntary sector and in the public sector, paying the going hourly rate for the job and earning the equivalent of their welfare payment and a small top-up[49].

## 3. On Participation:

- Introduce arenas where all stakeholders can discuss what needs to be done on different issues *on the basis of available evidence*. In these arenas evidence alone should be considered. Power differentials should not play a part.

- Introduce a process of social dialogue that includes all major sectors of Irish society on an equal basis. This process should focus on:

---

[49] *Social Justice Ireland* has made a comprehensive proposal on this issue, based on an identical programme it piloted for Government in the 1990s and which was subsequently mainstreamed successfully.

- the kind of Ireland people wish to see emerge in the future;
- the level of services and infrastructure to be provided;
- how these are to be funded, and
- how they are to be delivered.

Only then can fair choices be made on how Ireland's resources are to be used.

## 4. On Sustainability:

- Put sustainability at the centre of all policy-making. This requires an integrated approach to policy-development and Budget decision-making.
- Develop "satellite" or "shadow" national accounts that include a more comprehensive range of data than that currently included in GDP/GNP – such as the value of unpaid work and the cost of unsustainable development .

## 5. On measuring what matters:

- Ensure that data is collected on the various aspects of people's well-being, much of which is already being done in CSO publications such as 'Measuring Ireland's Progress'.
- Include these data in the policy development and implementation processes.

## 6. On health:

- Focus on addressing the social determinants of health as the basis for policy development.
- Prioritise and resource Primary Care Teams and Social Care with a major focus on prevention.
- Ensure that structural and systematic reform of the health system reflects the key principles of the Health Strategy aimed at achieving high performance, person centred, quality of care and value for money in the health service.

## 7. On education:

- Develop education as a life-long support helping people to become capable and emotionally well-rounded, happy and motivated.
- Address the social class inequities ingrained in formal education system at present.
- Address Ireland's large-scale adult literacy deficits.

## 8. On accommodation:

- Focus on developing housing as a home rather than as a market commodity.
- Ensure all people in Ireland have appropriate accommodation and thus eliminate all housing waiting lists.
- To this end ensure the supply of social housing including voluntary/non-profit and co-op housing on the scale required.

## 9. On cultures:

- Promote integration and an inclusive society.
- Respect the new cultures that have recently arrived in Ireland and ensure they are valued in Irish policy development.

## 10. On social capital, civil society, social well-being and active citizenship:

- Recognise and value the contribution currently being made to Ireland's development by the Community and Voluntary Sector.
- Develop active citizenship and social capital in a balanced way ensuring the required complementarity between the individual and society.

# Conclusion

The EU and the countries within it, including Ireland, need to have a wide-ranging dialogue on the future of the European Social Model. As outlined earlier in this chapter this dialogue should include all major stakeholders and sectors of society on an equal basis.

This process should focus on:

o   the kind of EU/Ireland people wish to see emerge in the future;
o   the level of services and infrastructure to be provided;
o   how these are to be funded, and
o   how they are to be delivered.

Then and only then can fair choices be made on what Social Model people wish to follow in the twenty first century and on how resources are to be used to deliver that model.

# References

Adema, W. And M. Ladaique, (2009) *How Expensive is the Welfare State?* OECD, France

Bryson, L. (1992) *Welfare and the State: Who Benefits?* Basingstoke, Macmillan.

Department of Social, Community and Family Affairs (2000), *Supporting Voluntary Activity*, Dublin, Stationery Office.

Esping-Andersen , G. (1990) *The Three Worlds of Welfare Capitalism*, Cambridge: Polity Press

European Commission (1994) *White Paper on Social Policy* (COM (94) 333), Brussels: EC

Farrell, C, H. McAvoy and J. Wilde (2008) *Tackling Health Inequalities: An All-Ireland Approach to Social Determinants*, Dublin: Institute of Public Health and Combat Poverty Agency.

*Gaudium et Spes, Pastoral Constitution on the Church in the Modern World*, 1965 accessed at: http://www.vatican.va/archive/hist_councils/ii_vatican_council/documents/vat-ii_cons_19651207_gaudium-et-spes_en.html

George, V. (2010) *Major Thinkers in Welfare: Contemporary Issues in Historical Perspective*, Bristol, The Policy Press.

Giddens, A. (2011) *Sociology*, Sixth edition, Cambridge: Polity Press

Healy, S. and Reynolds, B. (2009), *Beyond GDP: What is progress and how should it be measured?* Dublin: Social Justice Ireland

Healy, S. and Reynolds, B. (2008), *Making Choices, Choosing Futures*, Dublin: CORI Justice Commission.

Healy, S. and Reynolds, B. (2005), *Securing Fairness and Wellbeing in a Land of Plenty*, Dublin: CORI Justice Commission.

Healy, S. and B. Reynolds (2003), "Ireland and the Future of Europe – a social perspective" in Reynolds B. and S. Healy (eds.) *Ireland and the Future of Europe: leading the way towards inclusion?* Dublin, CORI.

Healy, S. and Reynolds, B. (1996), "Progress, Values and Public Policy" in Reynolds, B. and Healy, S. (eds.), *Progress, Values and Public Policy*, Dublin, CORI, pp. 11-59.

Healy, S. and Reynolds, B. (1993), "Work, Jobs and Income: Towards a new Paradigm" in Reynolds, B. and Healy S. (eds.), *New Frontiers for Full Citizenship*, Dublin: CMRS.

Jamrozik, A. (2001) *Social Policy in the Post-Welfare State*, Longman, Sydney.

Kitchin, R. Gleeson, J. Keaveney, K. & O' Callaghan, C. (2010), A Haunted Landscape: Housing and Ghost Estates in Post Celtic Tiger Ireland *Working Paper Series no. 59, National Institute for Regional and Spatial Analysis*, NUI Maynooth.

Leonard, P. (1997) *Postmodern Welfare: Reconstructing an Emancipatory Project*, Sage Publications, London.

Marshall, T. H. (1973) *Class, Citizenship and Social Development* (Westport, CN: Greenwood).

Mishra, R. (1990) *The Welfare State in Capitalist Society: Policies of Retrenchment and Maintenance in Europe, North America and Australia*, Harvester Wheatsheaf, Hemel Hempstead.

Morrone, A. (2009), The OECD Global Project on Measruing Progress and the challenge of assessing and measuring trust in B. Reynolds and S. Healy, *Beyond GDP: What is prosperity and how should it be measured?* Social Justice Ireland, Dublin.

National Economic and Social Council, (2009) Report 119 Vol. 1, *Well-being Matters: A Social Report for Ireland*, Dublin, NESC.

Orenstein, M.A. (2000) *How Politics and Institutions affect Pension Reform in Three Post-Communist Countries*, Policy Research Working Paper. Washington DC: World Bank.

Oyen, E. (1986) 'The Sociology of Social Security' Editorial introduction, *International Sociology*, vol 1, no 3, pp 21921.

Rawls, J. (1971) *A Theory of Justice*, Harvard University Press, Cambridge, Mass.

Reynolds, B., S. Healy, M. Collins (2010) *The Future of the Welfare State*, (Dublin: Social Justice Ireland)

Rys, V. (2010) *Reinventing social security worldwide: Back to essentials*, Bristol: The Policy Press.

Pierson, P. (1994) *Dismantling the Welfare State? Reagan, Thatcher and the Politics of Retrenchment*, Cambridge University Press, Cambridge.

Sen, A. (1999) *Development as Freedom.* Oxford University Press, Oxford.

Social Justice Ireland, (2010) *Building a Fairer Tax System: The working poor and the cost of refundable tax credits,* Dublin, Social Justice Ireland: Policy Research Series.

Thaler, R. H. And C. R. Sunstein, (2008) *Nudge: Improving Decisions About Health, Wealth, and Happiness.* Yale University Press: New Haven & London

Timonen, V. (2003) *Restructuring the Welfare State: Globalization and Social Policy Reform in Finland and Sweden,* Edward Elgar, Cheltenham.

Turner, B. S. (1990) 'Outline of a Theory of Citizenship' *Sociology,* 24 (2)

Wilkinson, R. and K. Pickett, (2009) *The Spirit Level: Why More Equal Societies Almost Always Do Better,* Penguin, London.

World Commission on Environment and Development, (1987) *Our Common Future,* Oxford University Press, Oxford.

World Health Organisation, (2011), World Conference on the Social Determinants of Health, *Rio Political Declaration on Social Determinants of Health,* WHO.

World Health Organisation, (2004) *Commission on the Social Determinants of Health (CSDH): Notes b the Secretariat, Document number EB115/35.* WHO: Geneva.